MEL BAY PRESENTS... *THE ORIGINAL*

YOU CAN TEACH YOURSELF®

PIANO CHORDS

Introduction

You Can Teach Yourself Piano Chords combines regular music notation with visual illustrations to give a clear picture of how to voice basic piano chords. It will take you through common chord progressions in all keys and in different inversions. Regardless of your skill level, you will soon be able to play an accompaniment for yourself or someone else. We highly recommended that you take a look at the appendix section, which will help clarify some basic music theory.

Using your favorite songs, try to implement the material learned in this book as soon as possible. It will help you experience for yourself the joy of creating music!

Best of Luck,

Per Danielsson & Mel Bay

1 2 3 4 5 6 7 8 9 0

Contents

Major/Minor Progressions Using Inversions

Chord and Bass Note

Open Voicings

Appendix

How to use this book

In order to use this book to its fullest potential you need to know a few things. Each keyboard diagram contains fingering, right and left hand indication, note names, chord name, key indication and middle C position.

Fingering: Each finger has a number. The thumbs are always number 1 and the pinkies number 5. The fingering is indicated below the keyboard diagram.

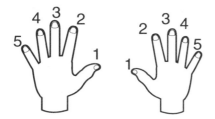

The notes under the **L:H** bracket should be played by the **Left Hand**.

The notes under the **R:H** bracket should be played by the **Right Hand**.

Note name indication:

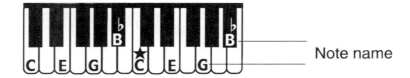

Note name

C Major

There are twelve major keys and twelve minor keys. All of the chords are shown in all keys. The key is indicated with a shadow box.

Middle C: Middle C is the reference point on the keyboard. Some electronic keyboards have middle C indicated but on regular pianos and grand pianos you have to find it yourself. It is located in the center of the keyboard, close to the key hole (if you have a piano that you can lock). In all the keyboard diagrams in this book, middle C is indicated by a star ★. Knowing the location of middle C is essential to placing the chord properly.

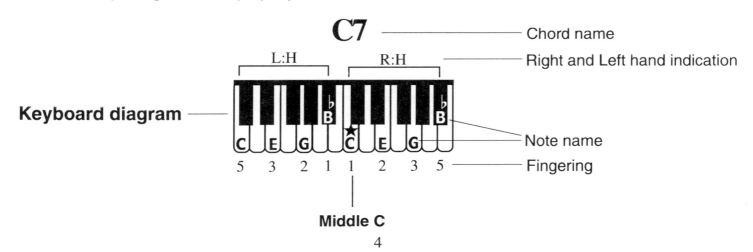

Middle C

4

C Major

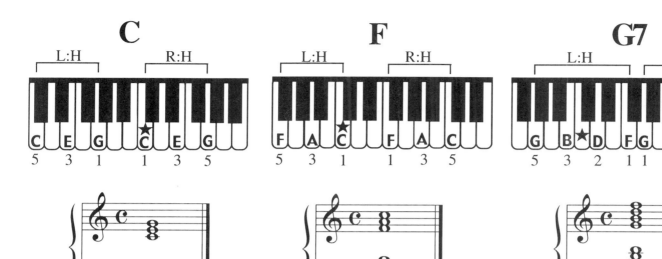

C Major Progression

A minor

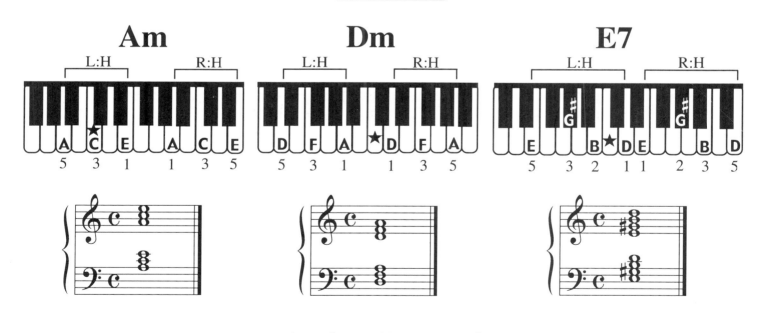

A minor Progression

F Major

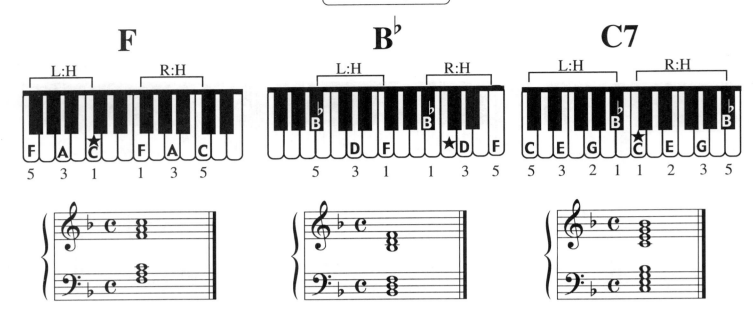

F Major Progression

D minor

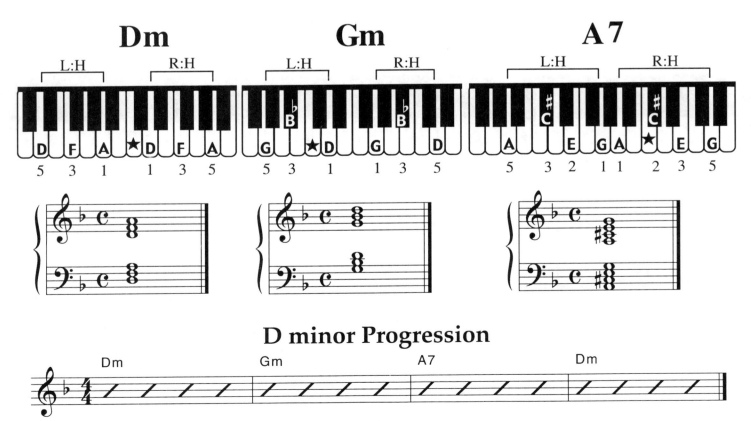

D minor Progression

B♭ Major

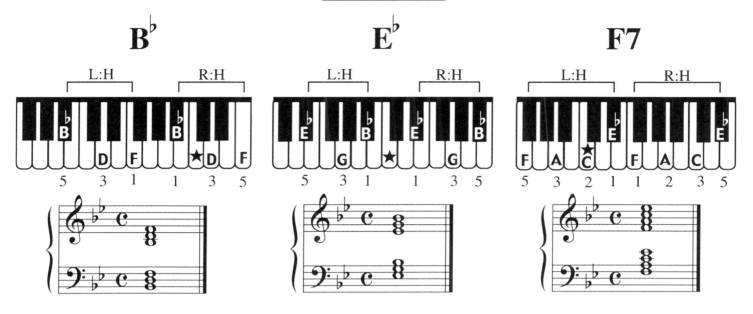

B♭ Major Progression

G minor

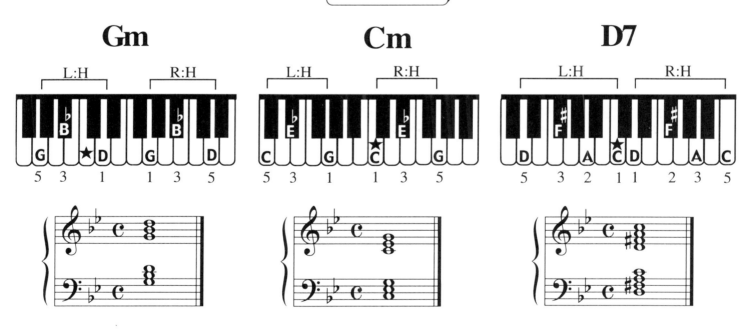

G minor Progression

E♭ Major

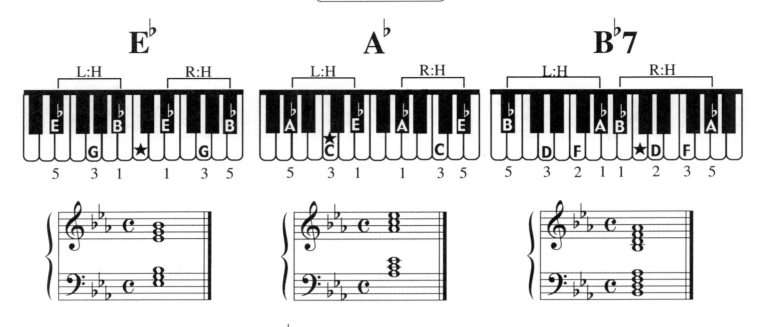

E♭ Major Progression

C minor

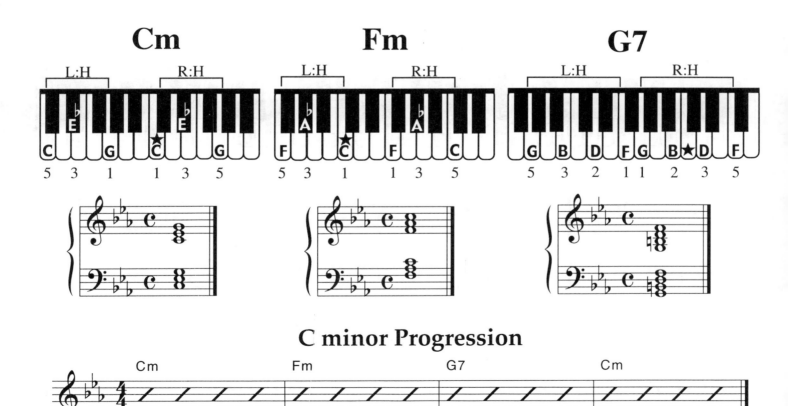

C minor Progression

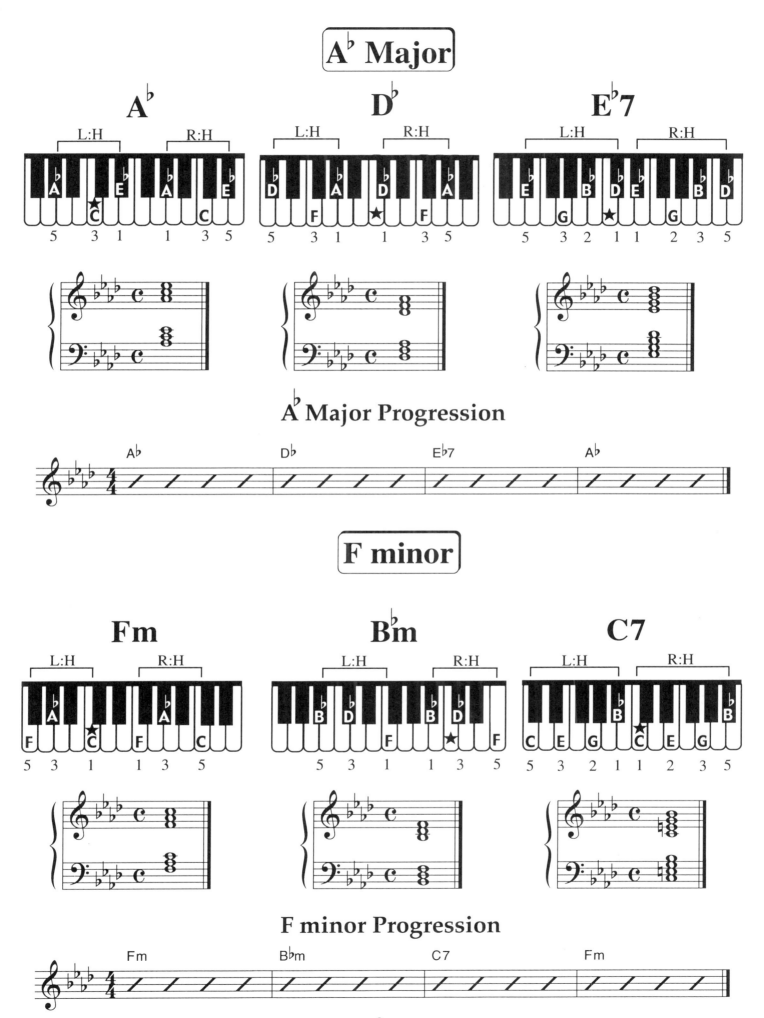

A♭ Major

A♭

D♭

E♭7

A♭ Major Progression

| A♭ | D♭ | E♭7 | A♭ |

F minor

Fm

B♭m

C7

F minor Progression

| Fm | B♭m | C7 | Fm |

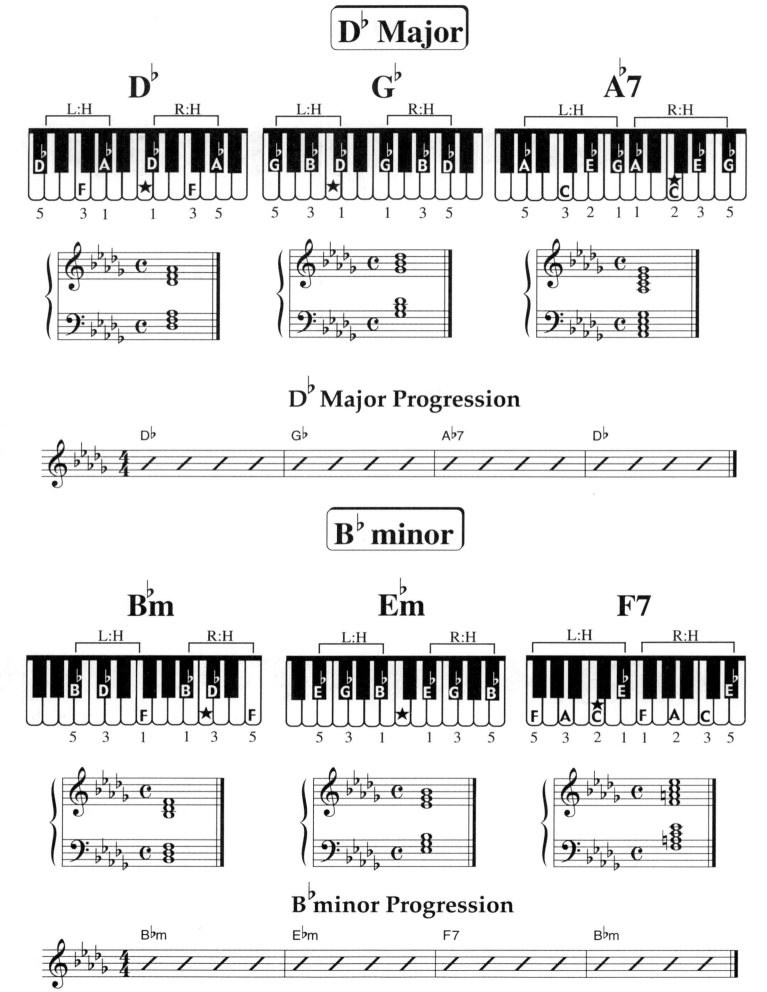

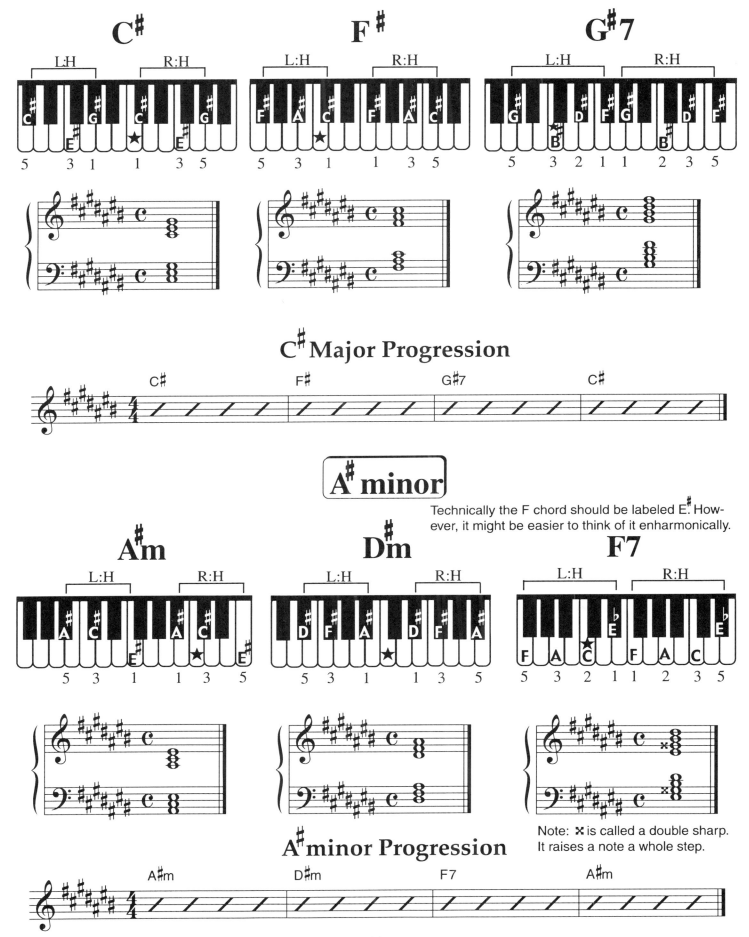

C# Major

C#
F#
G#7

C# Major Progression

C#　　　　F#　　　　G#7　　　　C#

A# minor

Technically the F chord should be labeled E#. However, it might be easier to think of it enharmonically.

A#m
D#m
F7

Note: ✕ is called a double sharp. It raises a note a whole step.

A# minor Progression

A#m　　　　D#m　　　　F7　　　　A#m

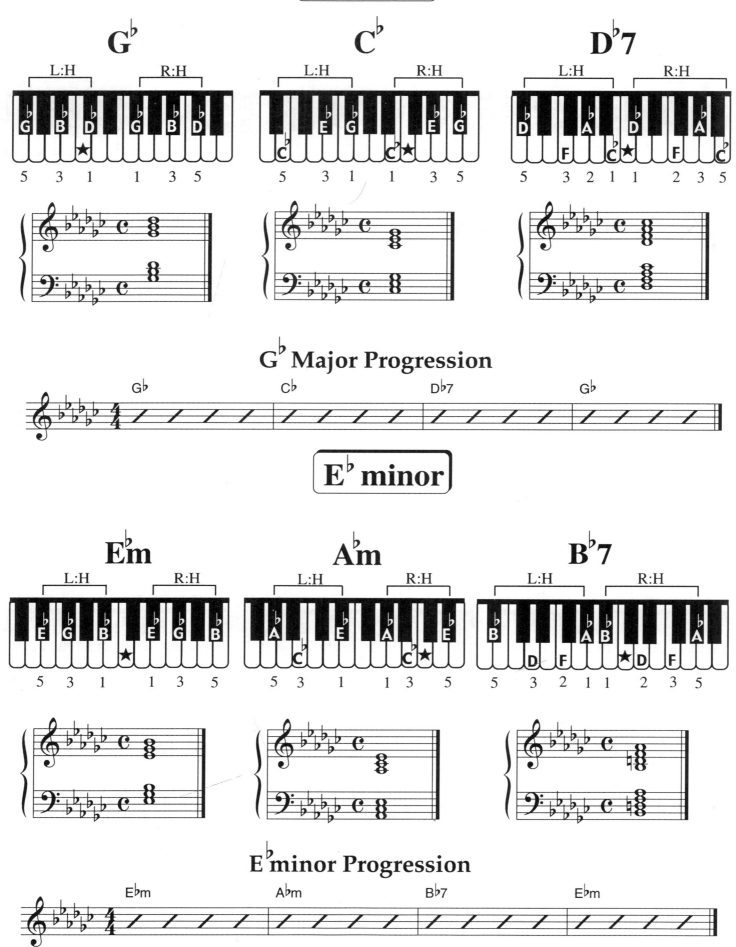

F#Major

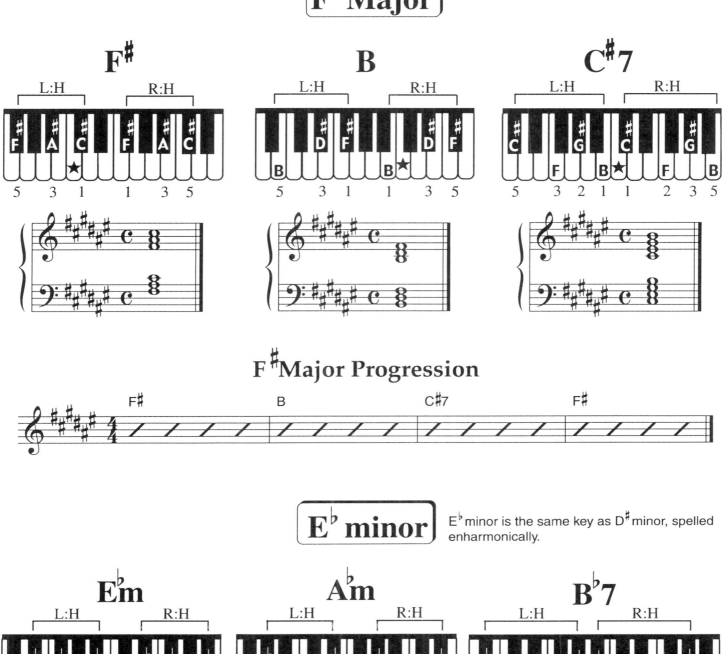

F#Major Progression

Eb minor

Eb minor is the same key as D#minor, spelled enharmonically.

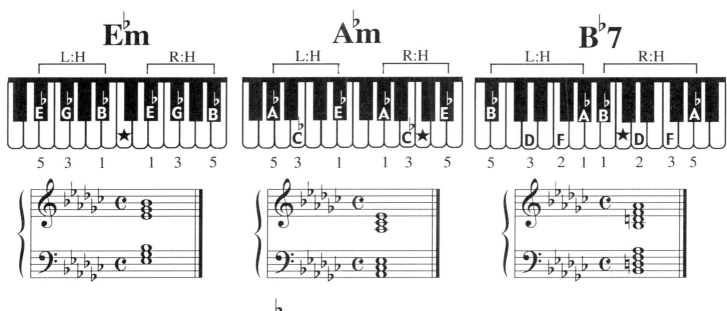

Eb minor Progression

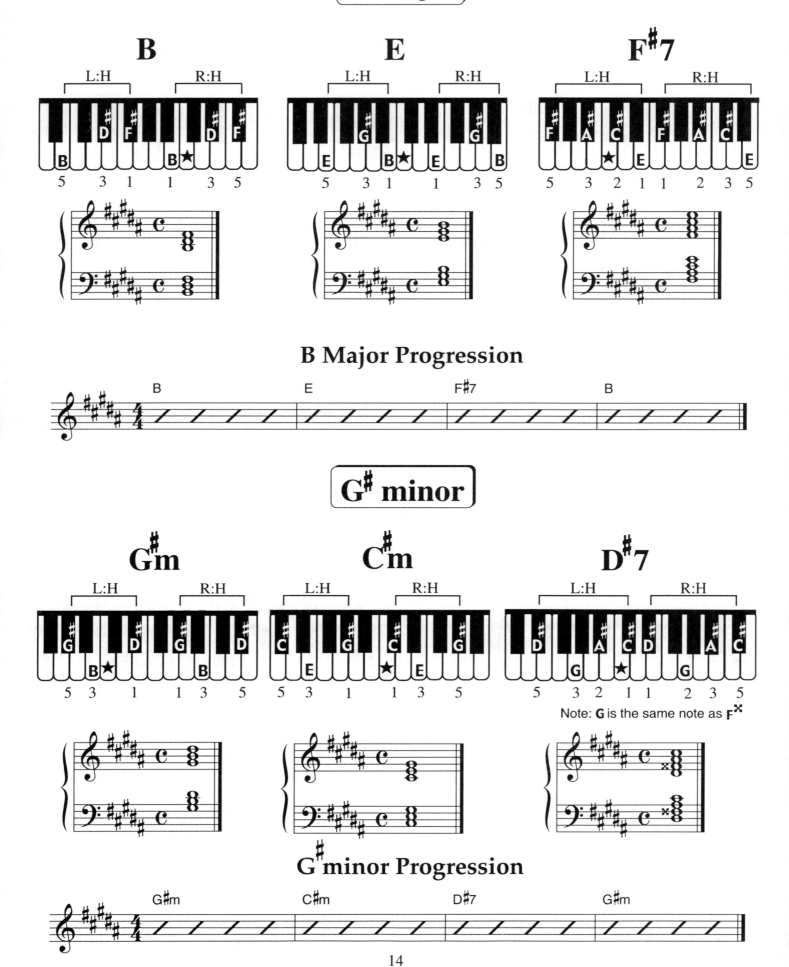

B Major

B **E** **F#7**

B Major Progression

B   E   F#7   B

G# minor

G#m **C#m** **D#7**

Note: **G** is the same note as **F×**

G# minor Progression

G#m   C#m   D#7   G#m

14

E Major

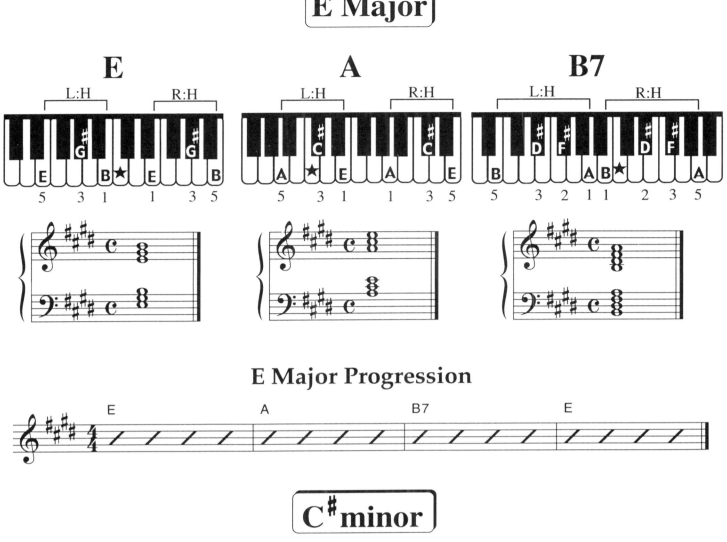

E Major Progression

| E | A | B7 | E |

C#minor

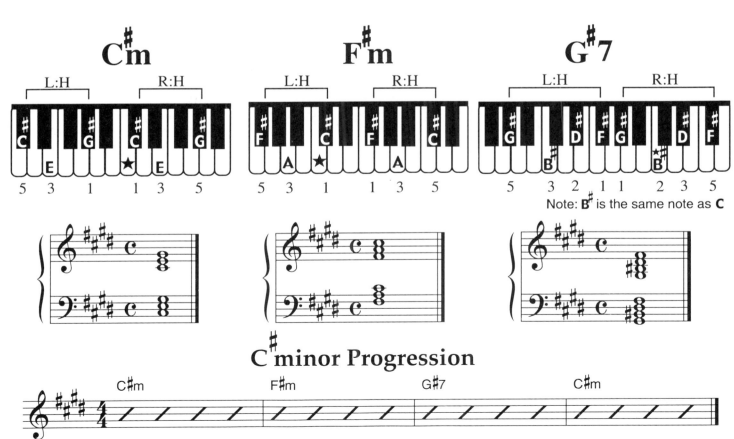

Note: **B#** is the same note as **C**

C#minor Progression

| C#m | F#m | G#7 | C#m |

A Major

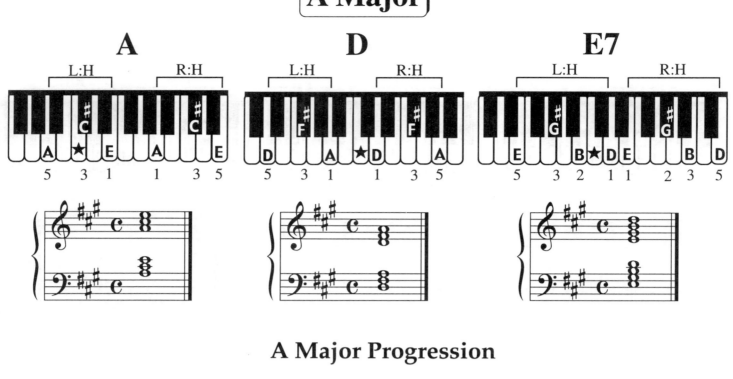

A Major Progression

| A | D | E7 | A |

F# minor

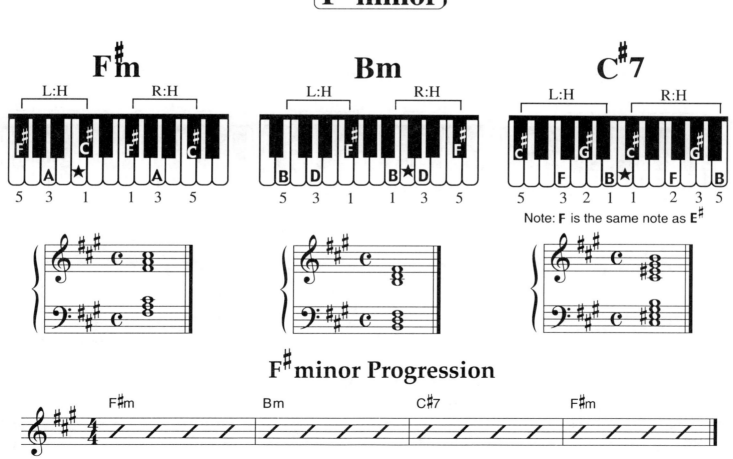

Note: F is the same note as E#

F# minor Progression

| F#m | Bm | C#7 | F#m |

D Major

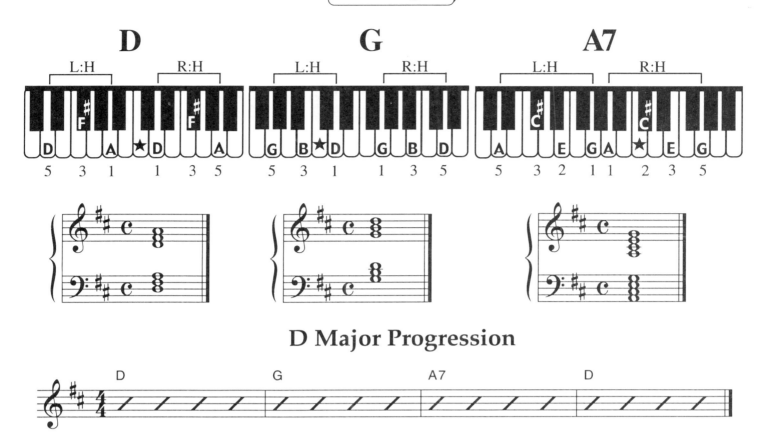

D Major Progression

D	G	A7	D

B minor

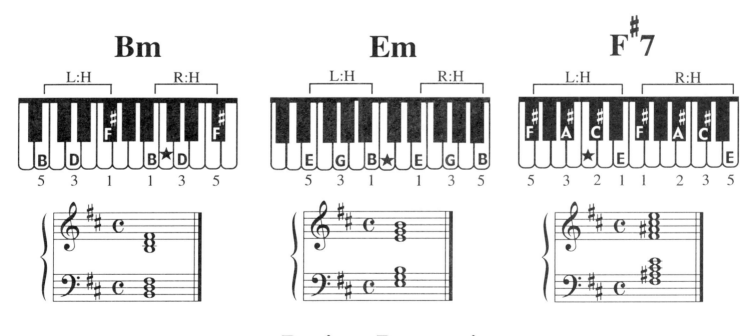

B minor Progression

Bm	Em	F#7	Bm

G Major

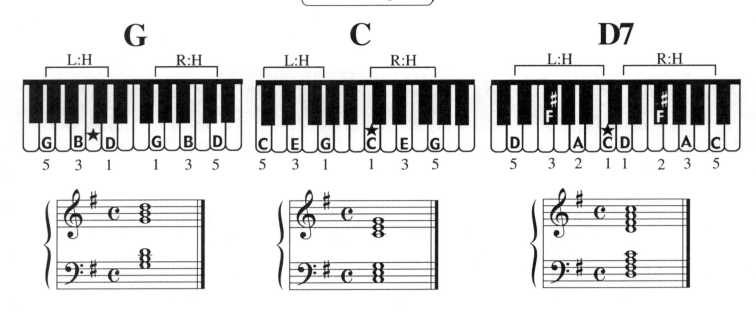

G Major Progression

E minor

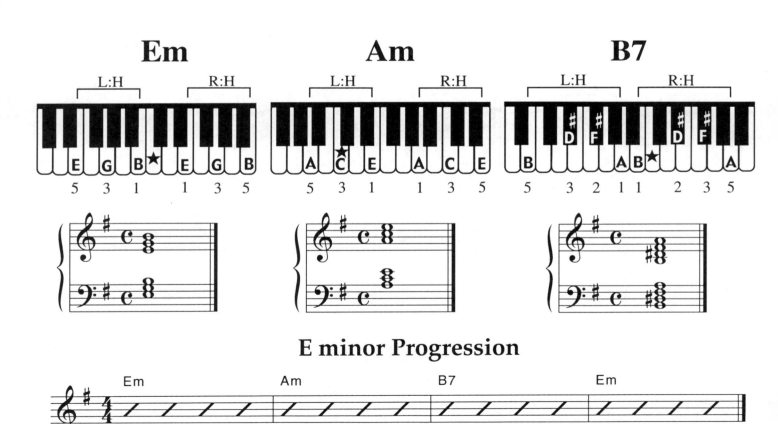

E minor Progression

18

Exercise Progressions

There are no key signatures indicated in the exercise progressions. Instead accidentals are used to spell out the correct chord. The goal with these exercises is to practice reading chord changes and develop speed. Start slowly and do not speed the tempo up until you feel secure with the chords. Practice the chords in different octaves.

Major chord in 4ths

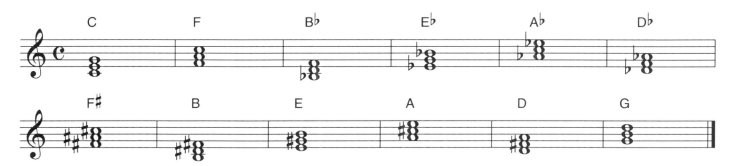

Major chromatically

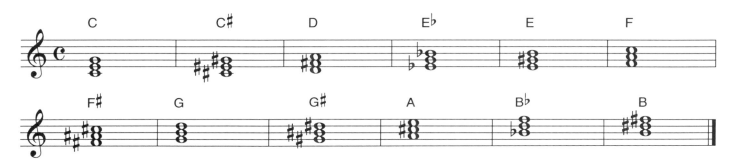

Minor chord in 4ths

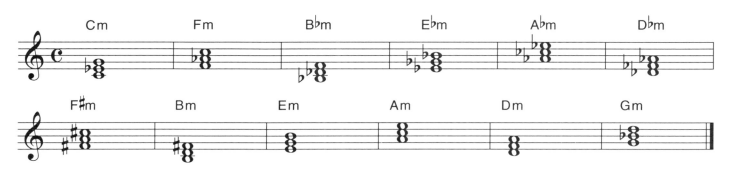

Minor chromatically

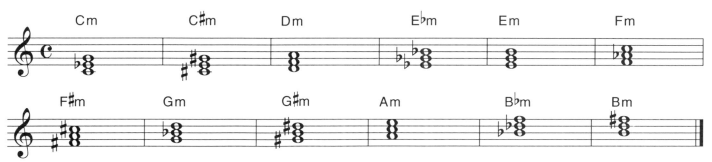

Dominant 7 chords in 4ths

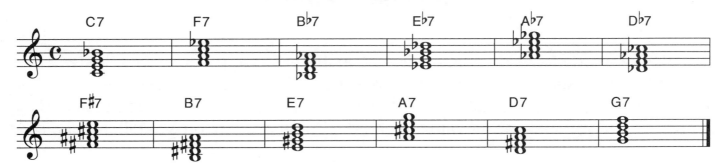

Dominant 7 chords chromatically

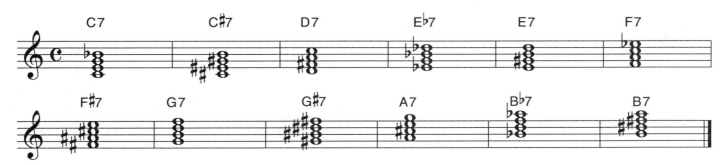

Major Progression

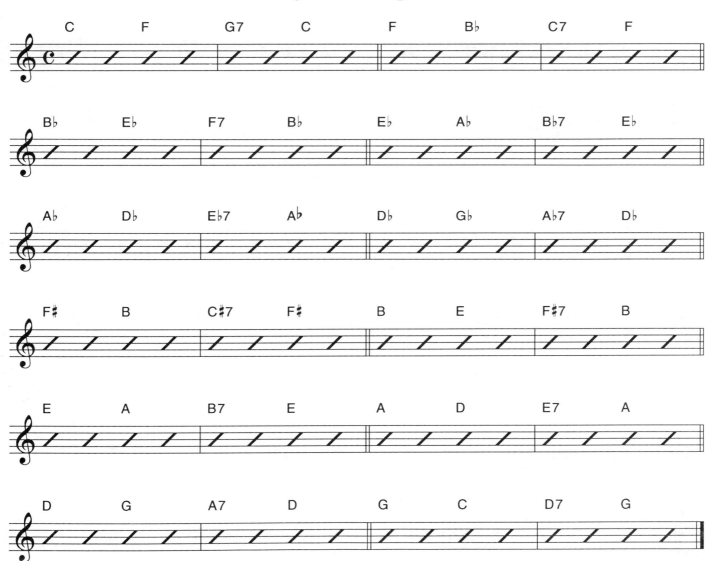

Minor Progression

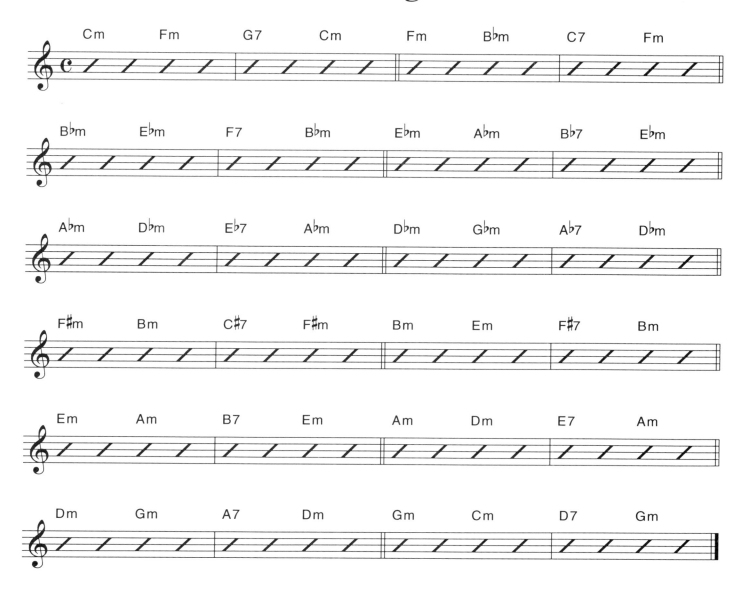

Inversions

You have now learned all the major triads, minor triads and dominant seventh chords in root position. The next step is to be able to play the inversions of these chords. In an inversion of a chord, the only thing that changes is the order of the notes. Since a triad consists of three notes, there are three different ways of organizing the notes, **root position, first inversion and second inversion.** The dominant seventh chord is made up of four notes so it has four combinations, **root position, first inversion, second inversion and third inversion.**

This is how inversions work:

To get the 1st inversion, take the bottom note of the chord and move it up one octave, while keeping the second and the third note the same. To get the second inversion, move the bottom note of the 1st inversion chord up an octave. Below you can see the different combinations of the inversions.

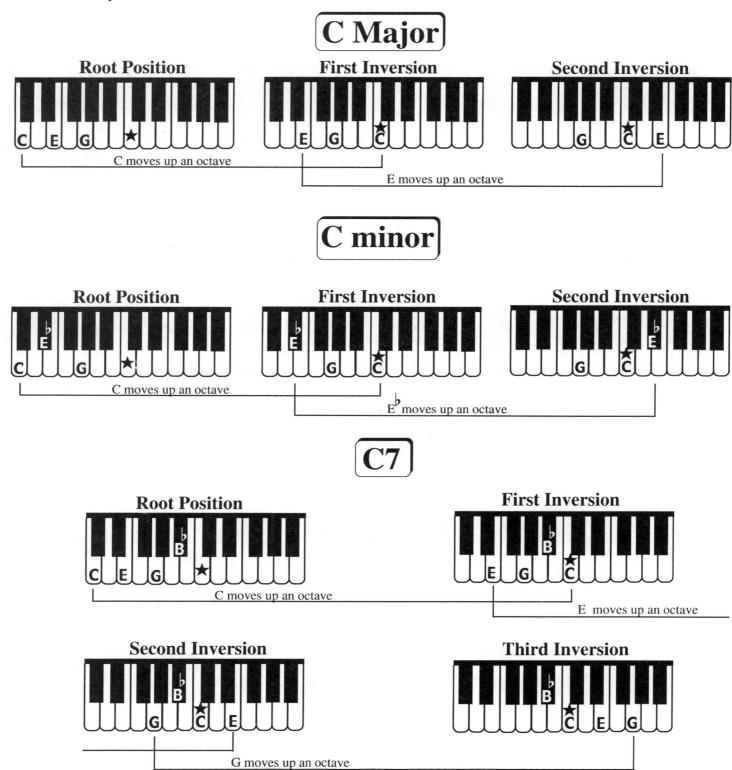

22

Major Triad Inversions

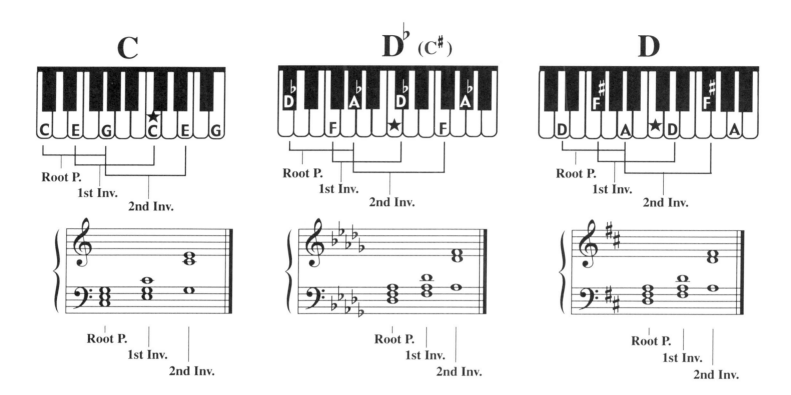

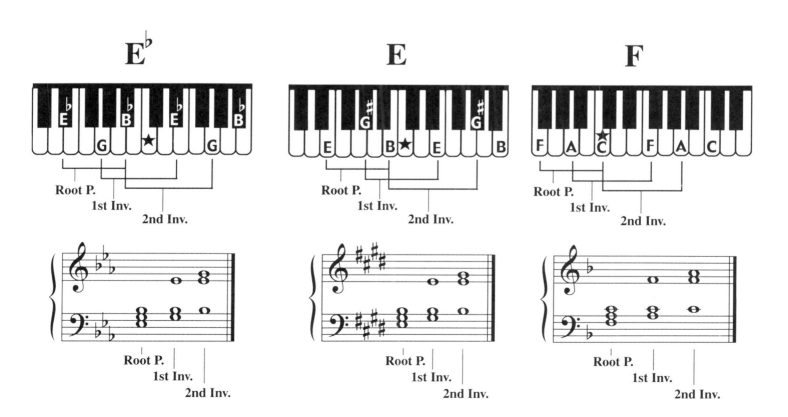

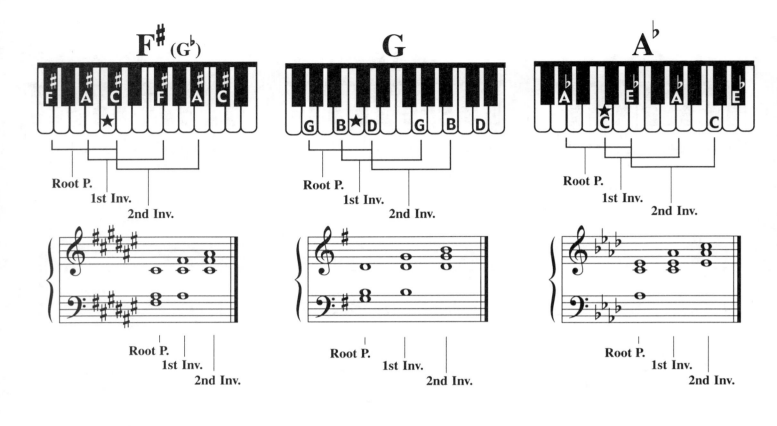

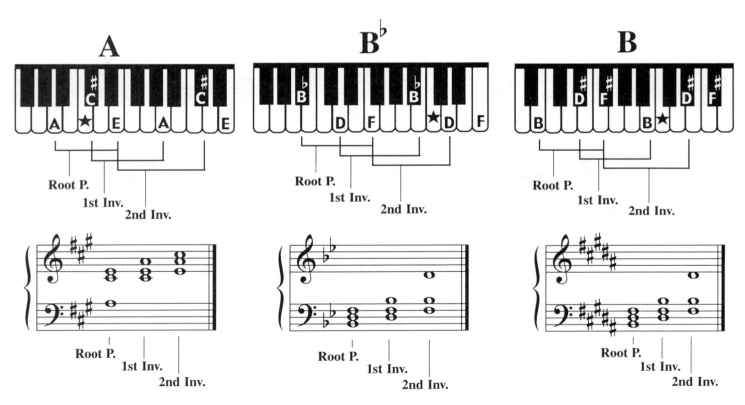

Minor Triad Inversions

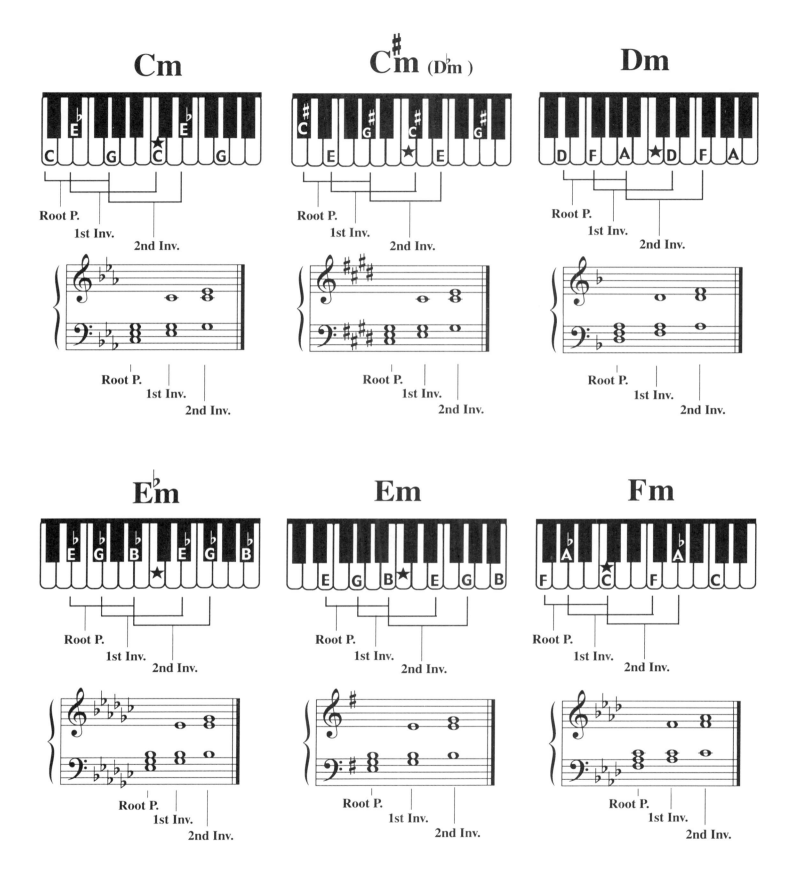

25

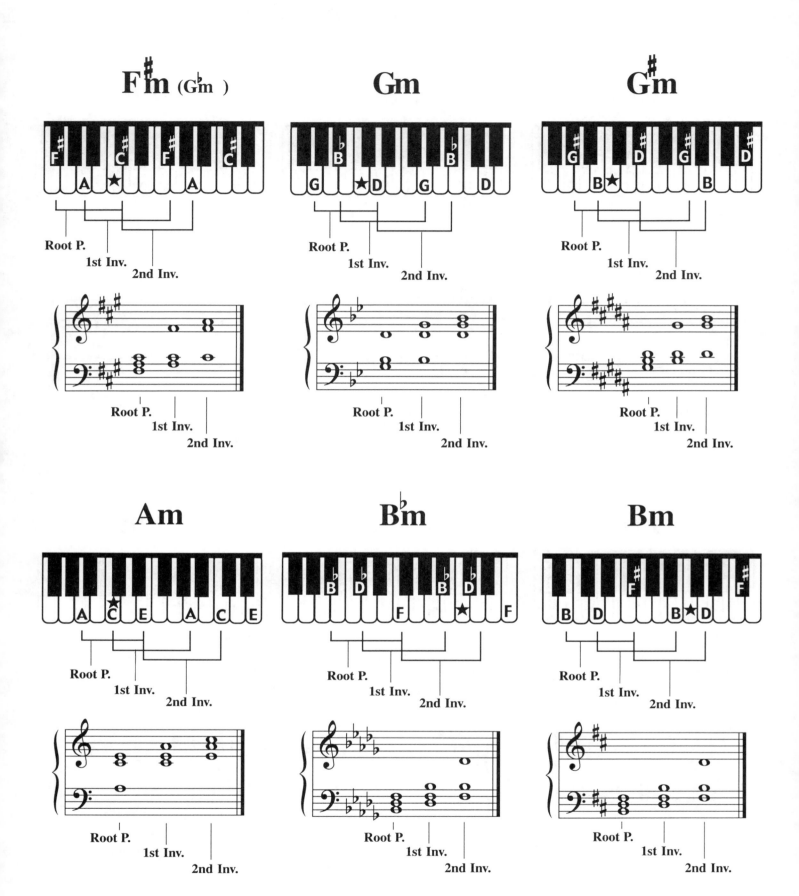

Dominant 7 Chord Inversions

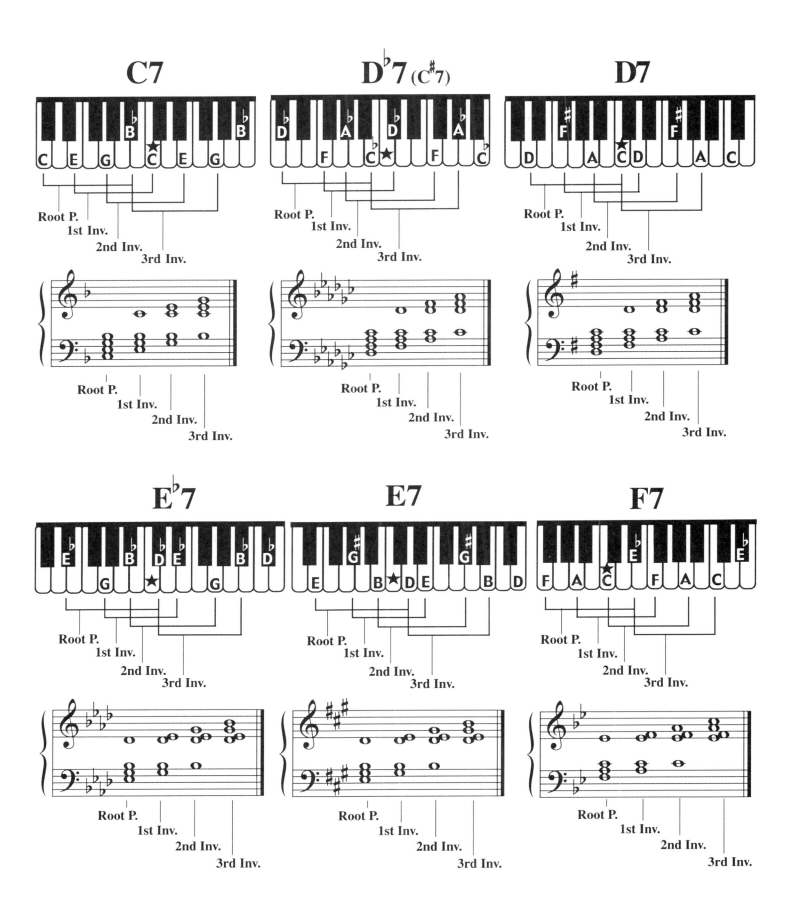

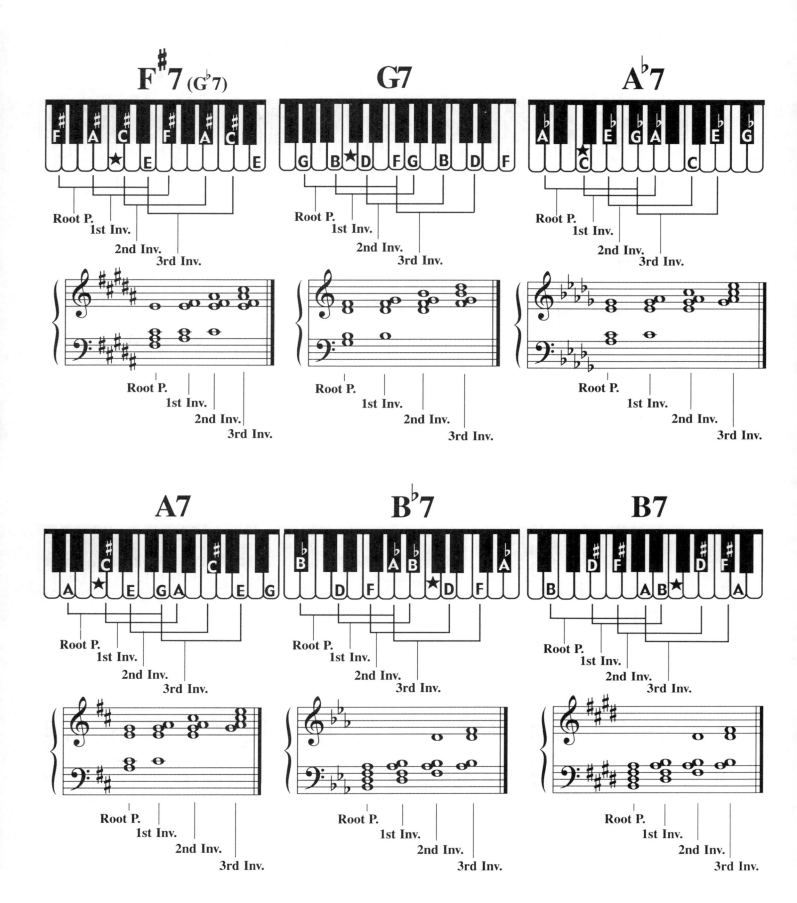

28

Major/Minor Progressions Using Inversions

C Major

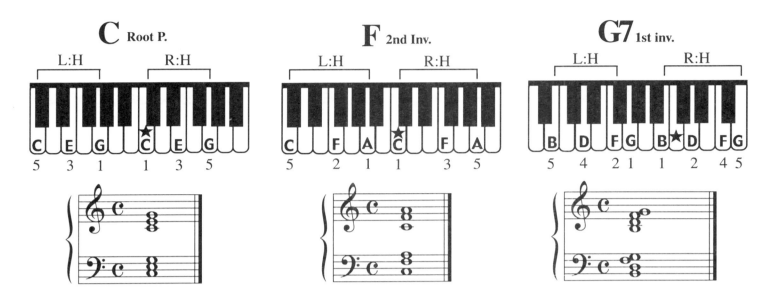

C Major Progression

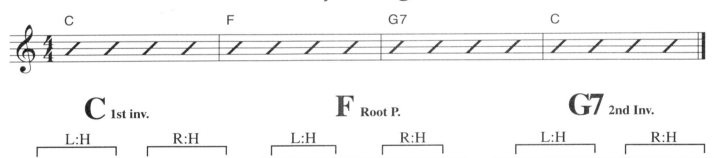

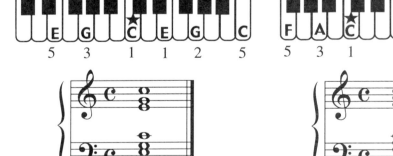
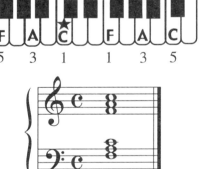
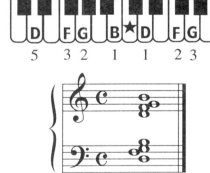

C Major Progression

C minor

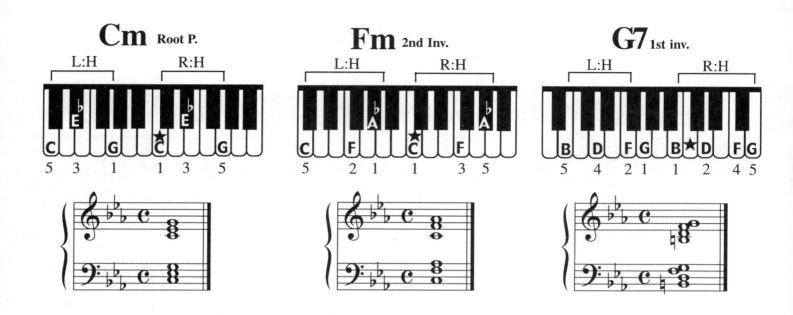

C minor Progression

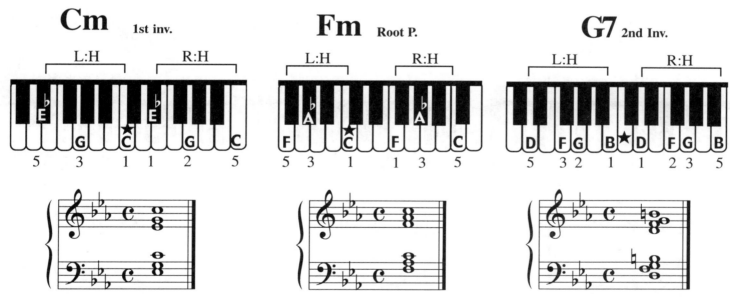

C minor Progression

F Major

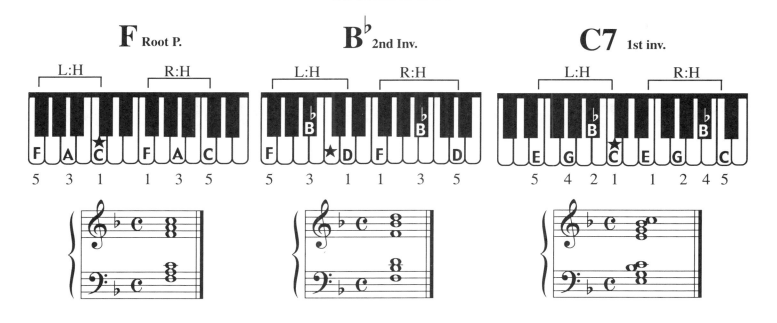

F Major Progression

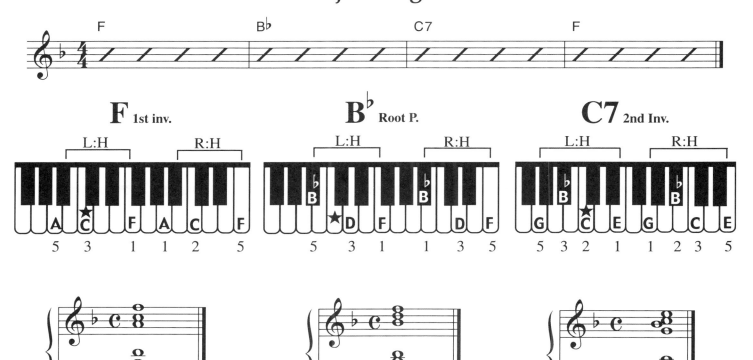

F Major Progression

F minor

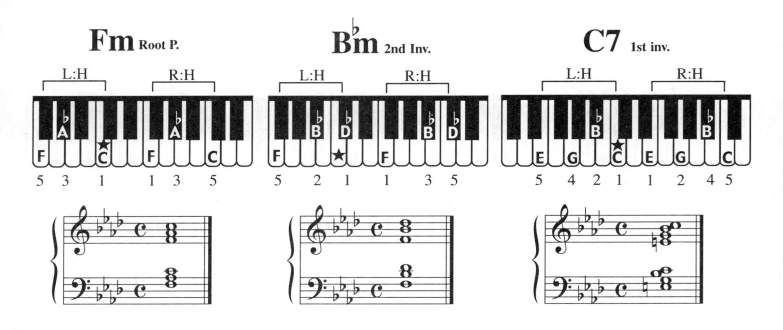

F minor Progression

| Fm | B♭m | C7 | Fm |

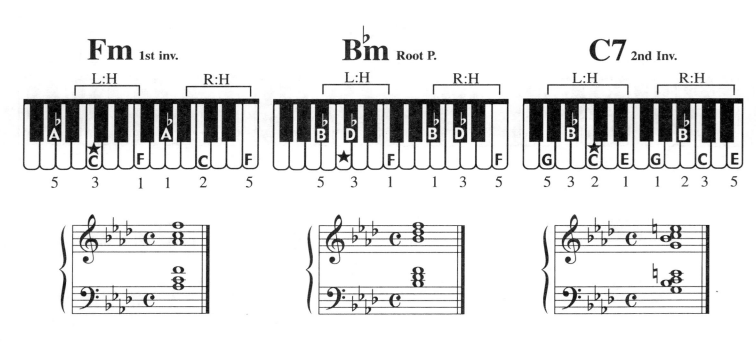

F minor Progression

| Fm | B♭m | C7 | Fm |

32

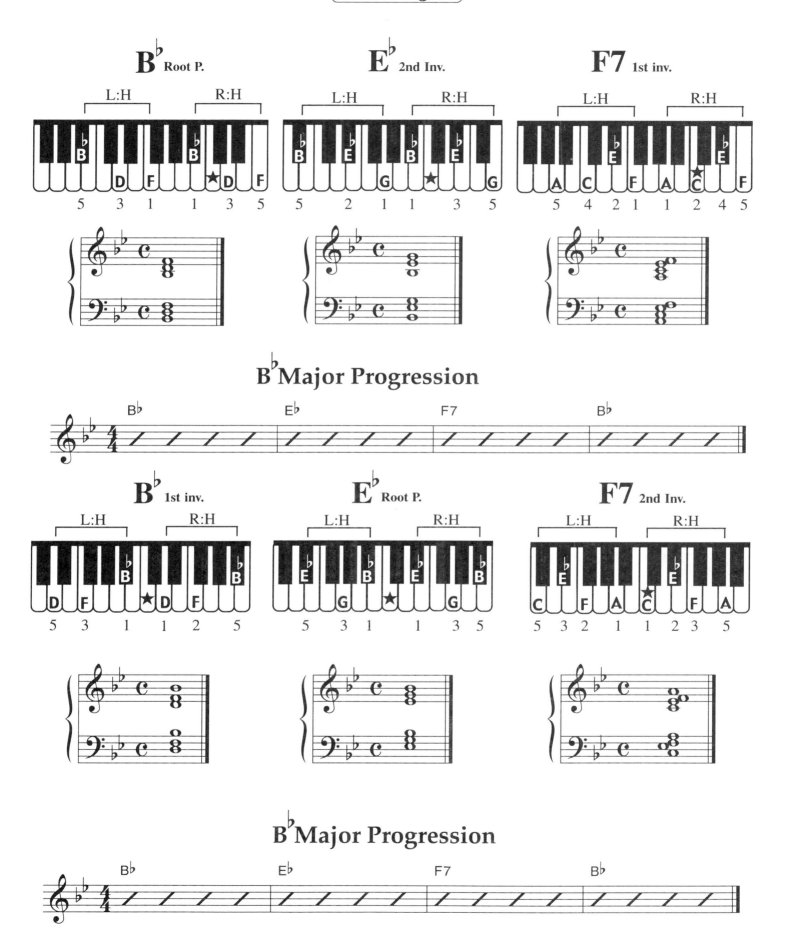

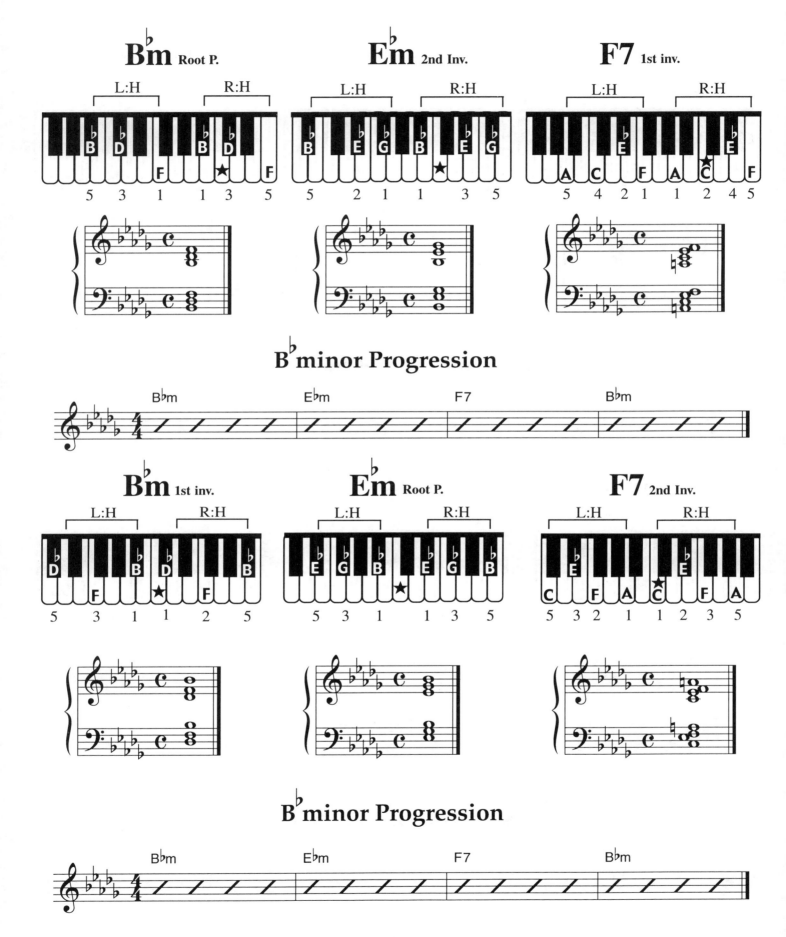

34

E♭ Major

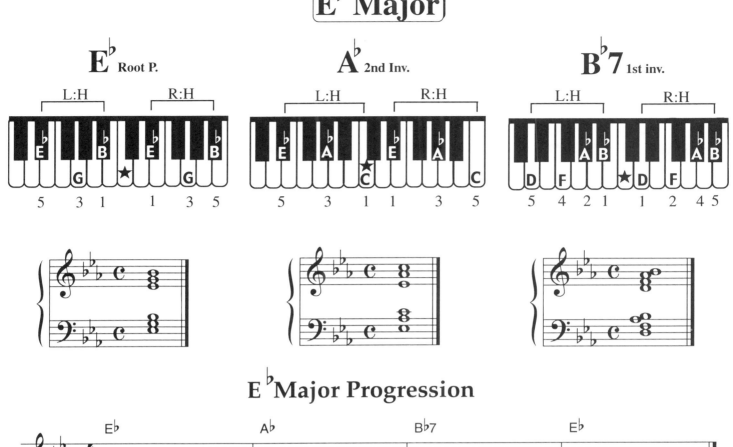

E♭ Major Progression

E♭ Major Progression

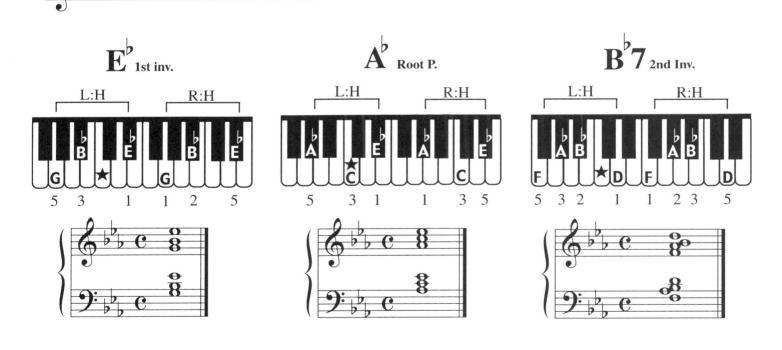

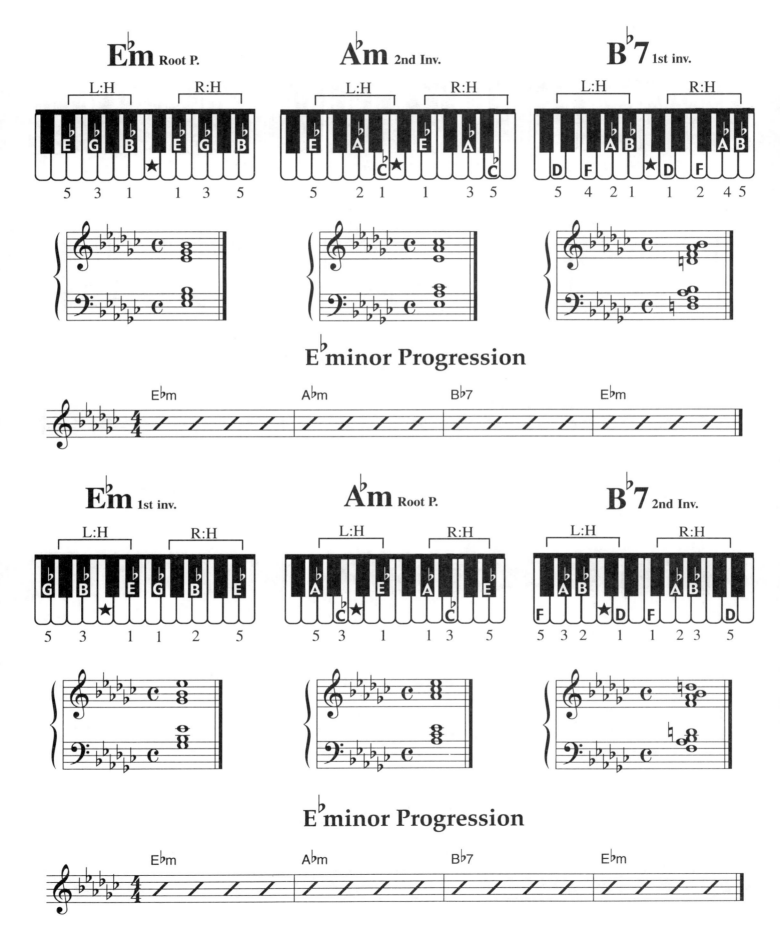

E♭ minor

36

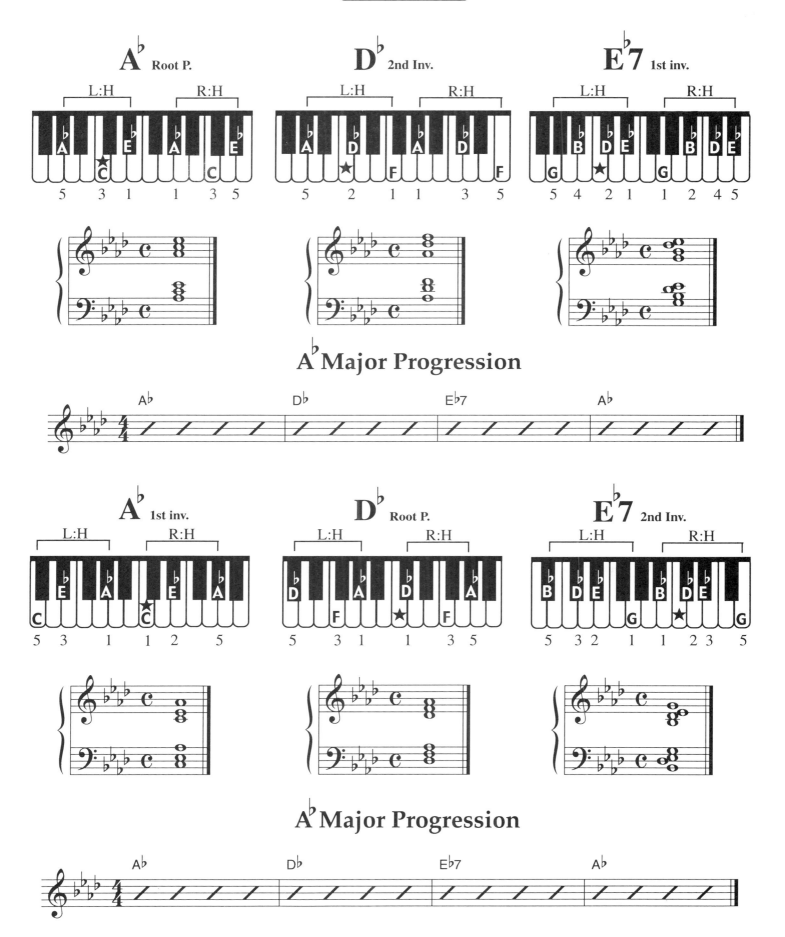

A♭ minor

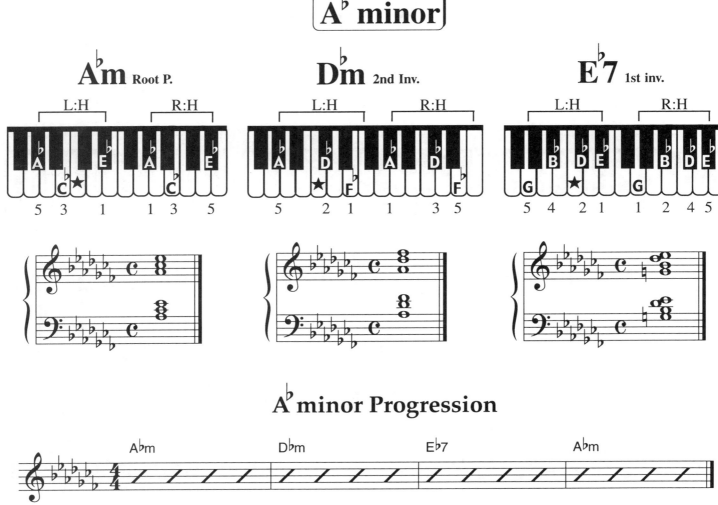

A♭m Root P.
D♭m 2nd Inv.
E♭7 1st inv.

A♭ minor Progression

| A♭m | D♭m | E♭7 | A♭m |

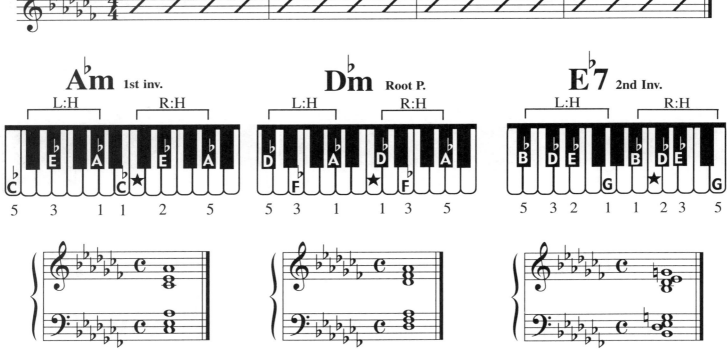

A♭m 1st inv.
D♭m Root P.
E♭7 2nd Inv.

A♭ minor Progression

| A♭m | D♭m | E♭7 | A♭m |

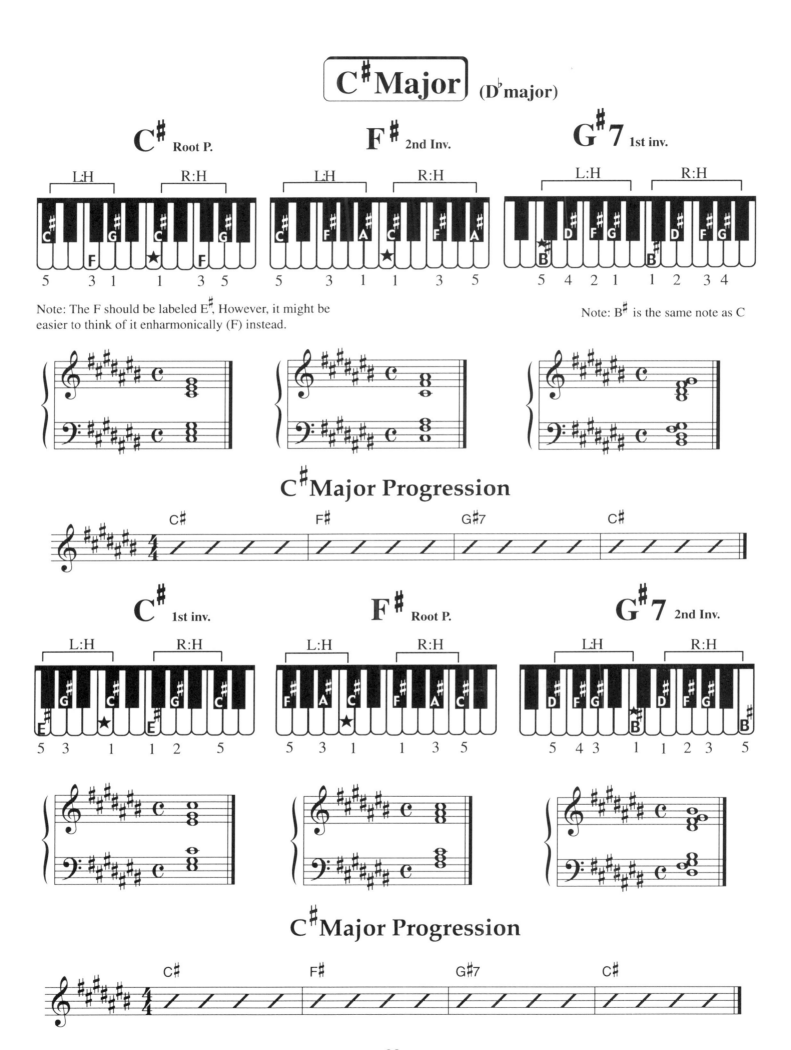

C# Major (D♭ major)

C# Root P.

Note: The F should be labeled E#, However, it might be easier to think of it enharmonically (F) instead.

F# 2nd Inv.

G# 7 1st inv.

Note: B# is the same note as C

C# Major Progression

| C# | F# | G#7 | C# |

C# 1st inv.

F# Root P.

G# 7 2nd Inv.

C# Major Progression

| C# | F# | G#7 | C# |

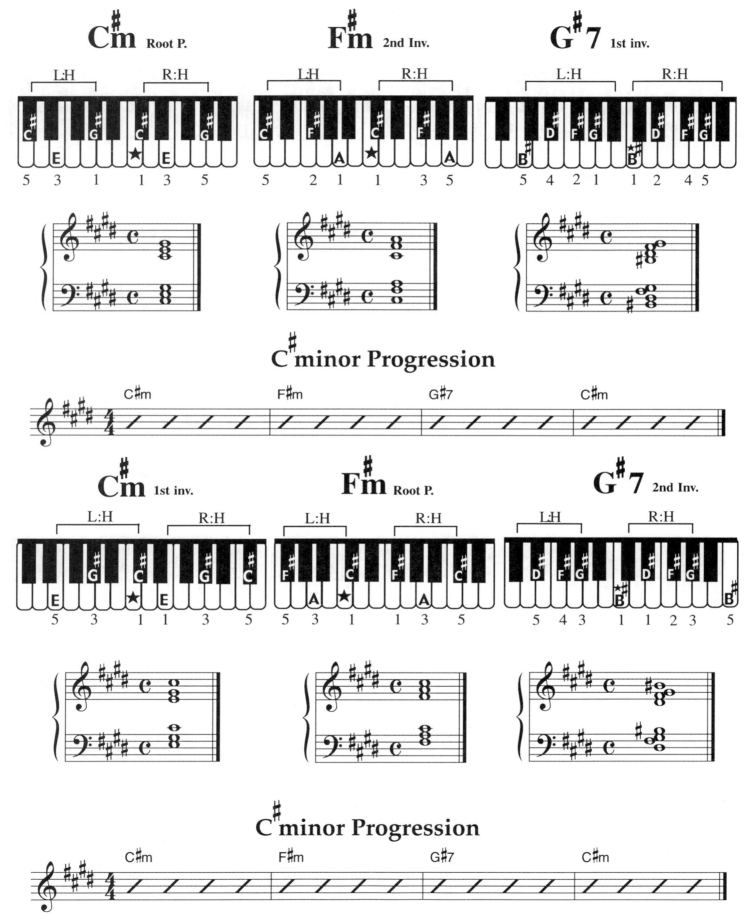

C#minor

Cm Root P.   **Fm 2nd Inv.**   **G#7 1st inv.**

C#minor Progression

C#m   F#m   G#7   C#m

Cm 1st inv.   **Fm Root P.**   **G#7 2nd Inv.**

C#minor Progression

C#m   F#m   G#7   C#m

G♭ Major (F#Major)

G♭ Root P.
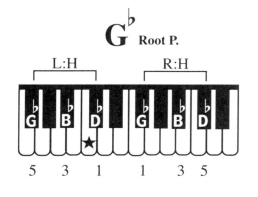

C♭ 2nd Inv.
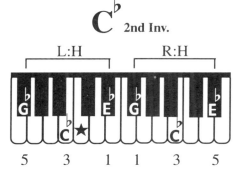

D♭7 1st inv.
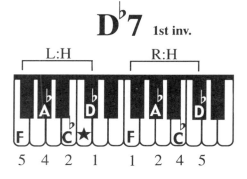

G♭ Major Progression

G♭ 1st inv.
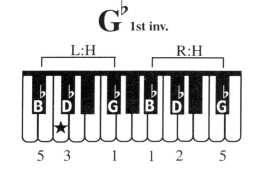

C♭ Root P.
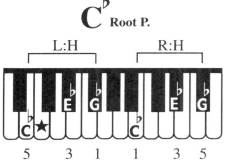

D♭7 2nd Inv.
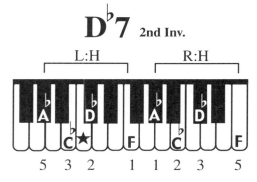

G♭ Major Progression

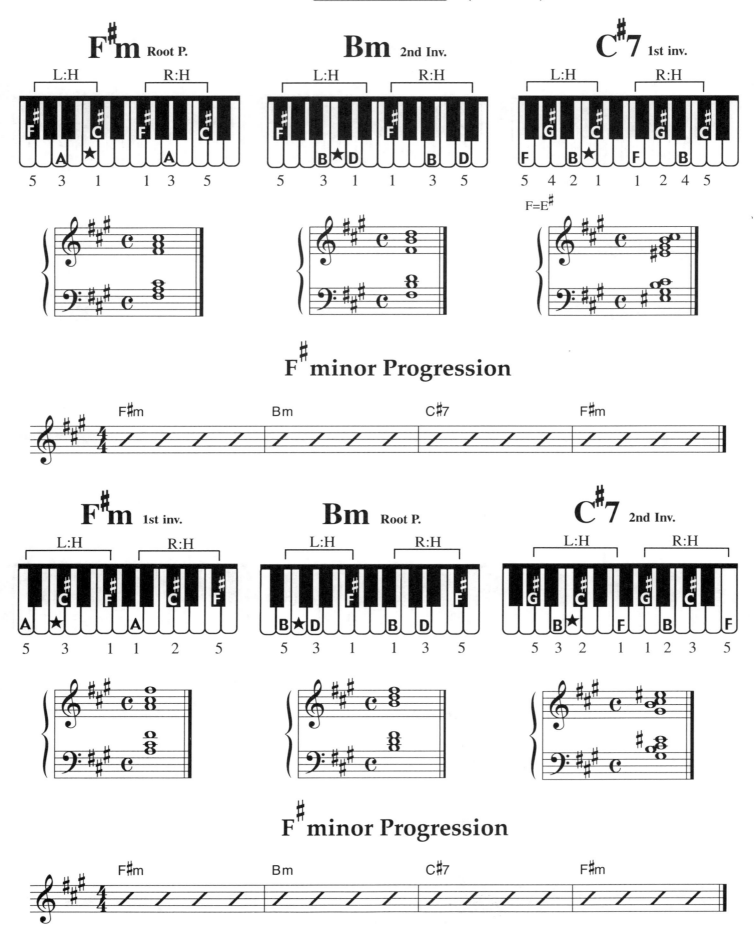

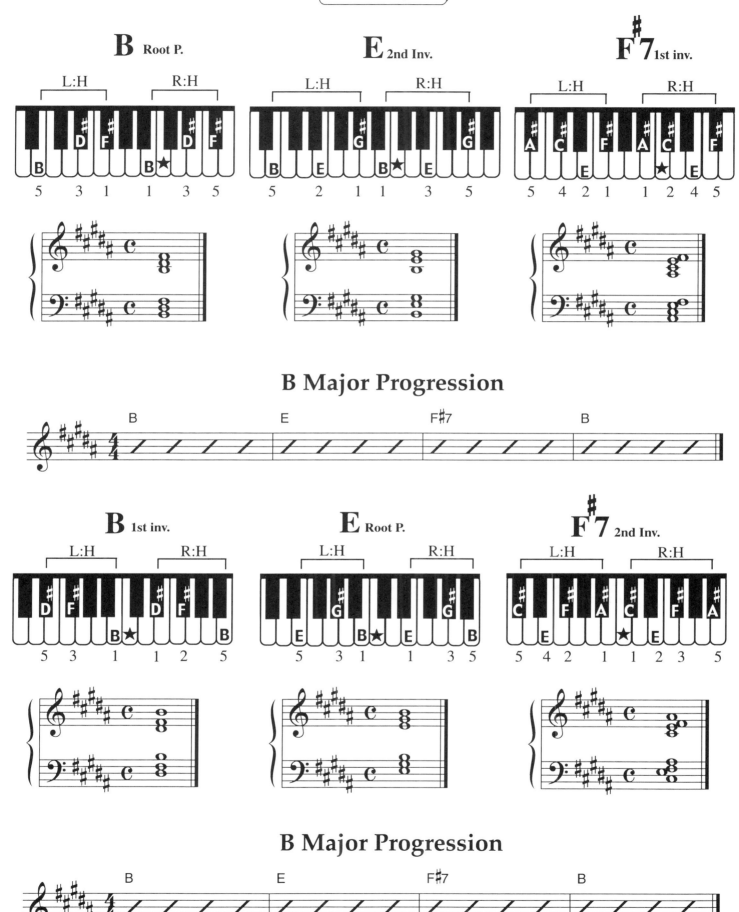

B Major

B Major Progression

B Major Progression

B minor

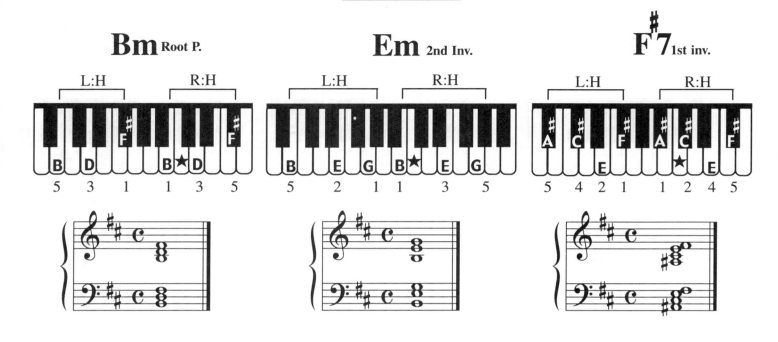

B minor Progression

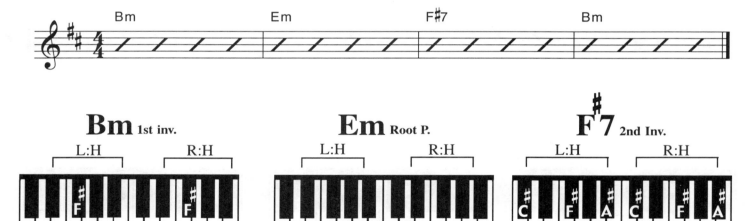

B minor Progression

E Major

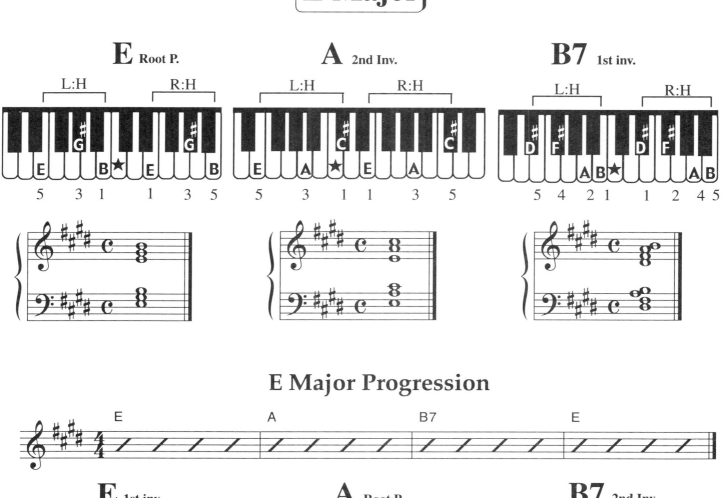

E Major Progression

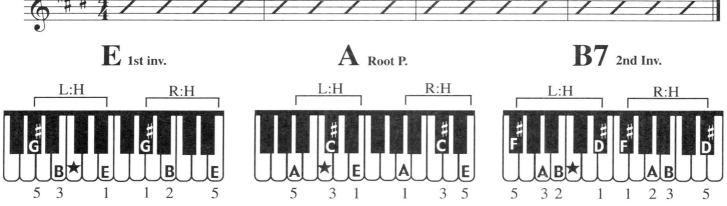

E Major Progression

E minor

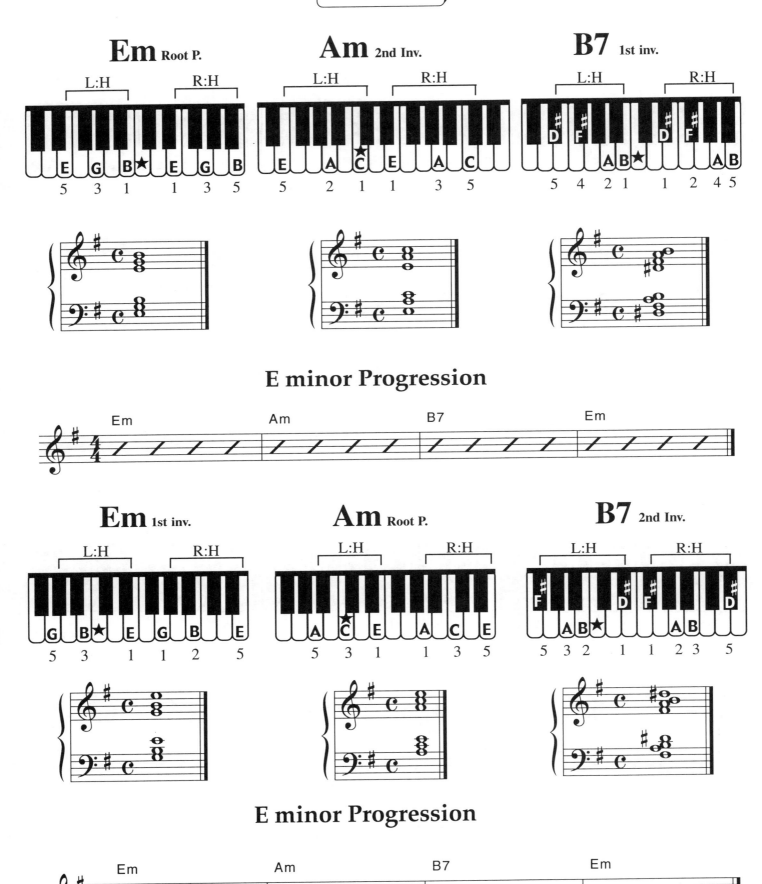

E minor Progression

E minor Progression

A Major

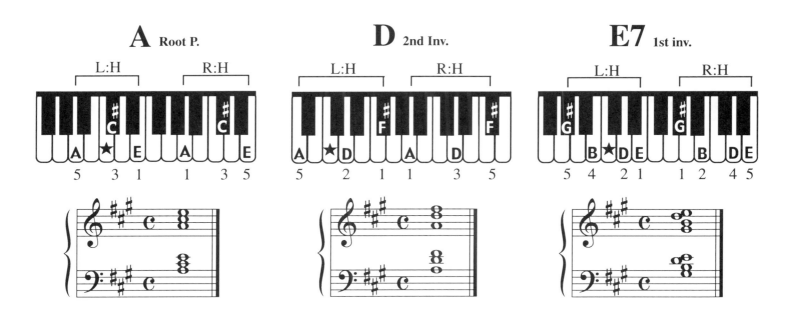

A Major Progression

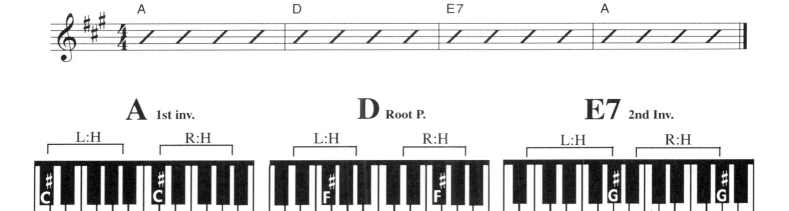

A Major Progression

A minor

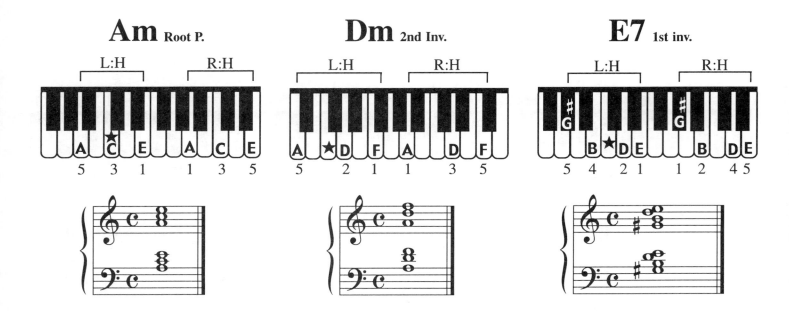

Am Root P.

Dm 2nd Inv.

E7 1st inv.

A minor Progression

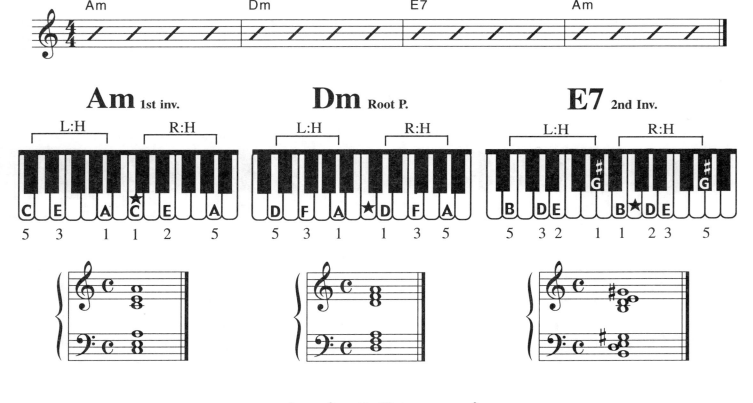

Am 1st inv.

Dm Root P.

E7 2nd Inv.

A minor Progression

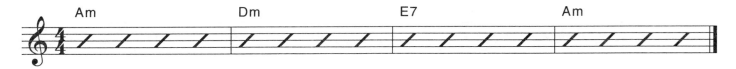

D Major

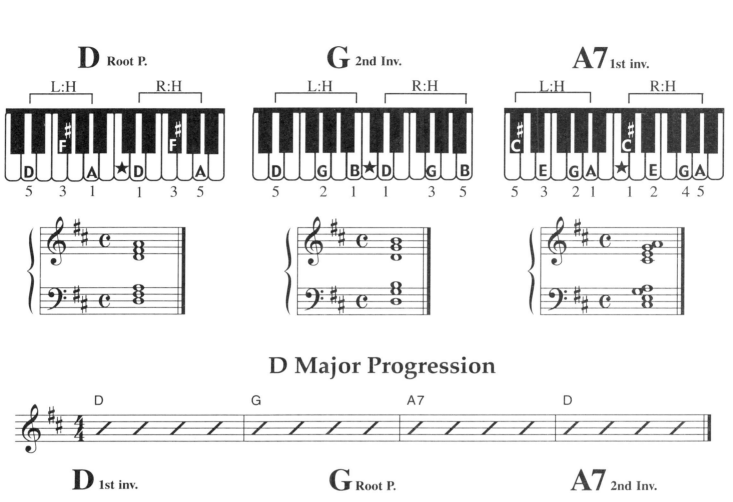

D Major Progression

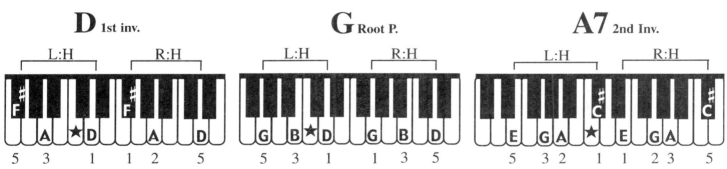

D Major Progression

49

D minor

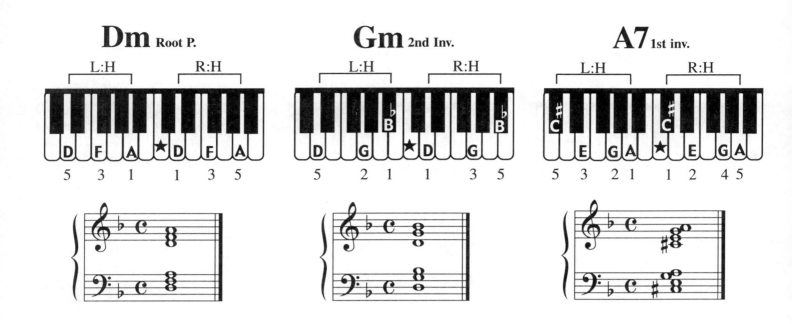

D minor Progression

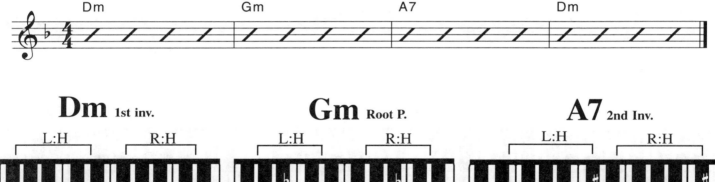

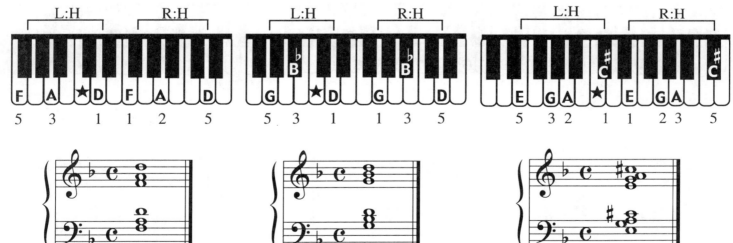

D minor Progression

G Major

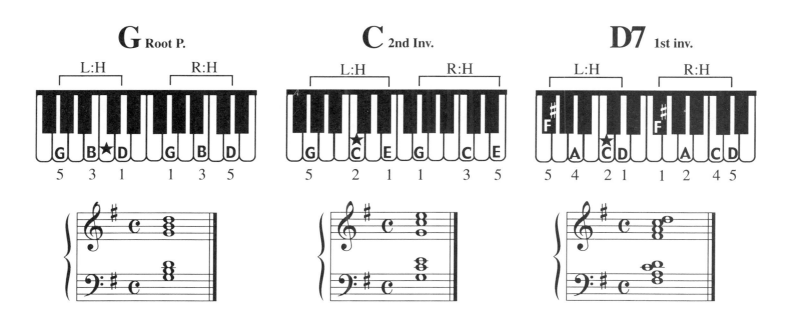

G Major Progression

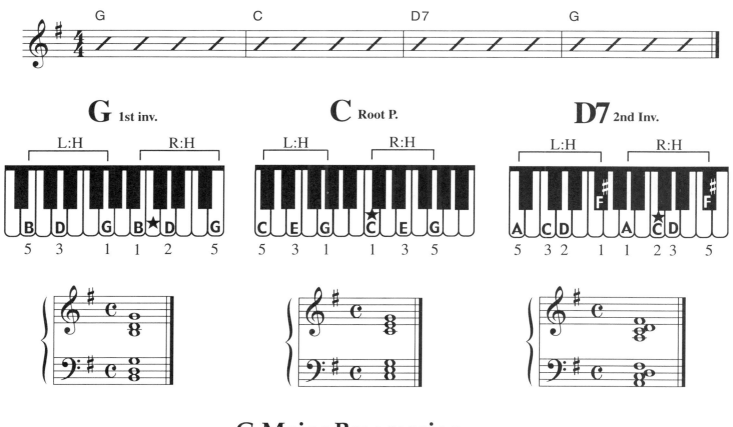

G Major Progression

G minor

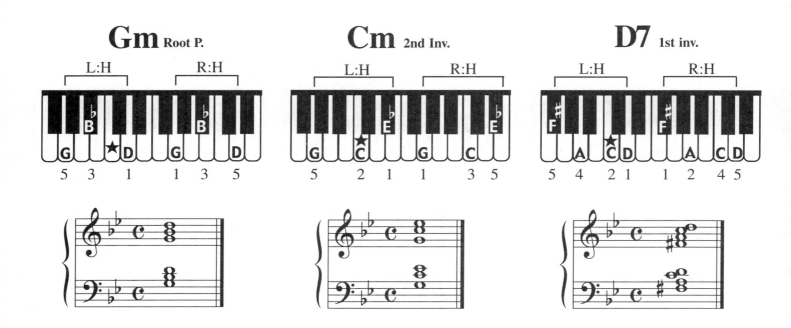

G minor Progression

Gm	Cm	D7	Gm

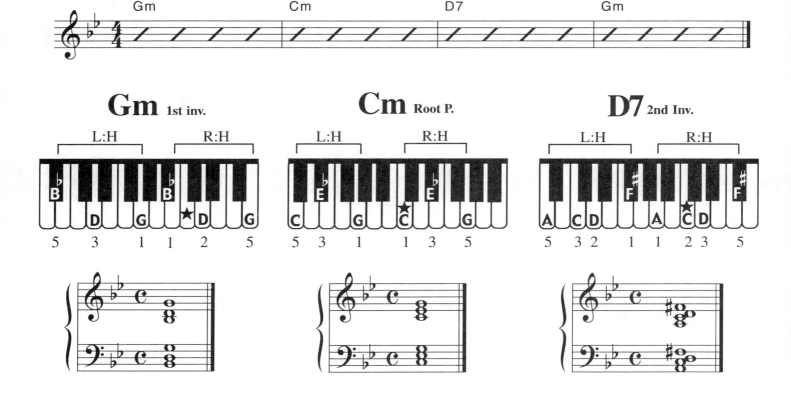

G minor Progression

Gm	Cm	D7	Gm

Major Key Progression

Major Key Progression

Blank Staff

It might be helpful to write in the inversions.

Minor Key Progression

Minor Key Progression
Blank Staff

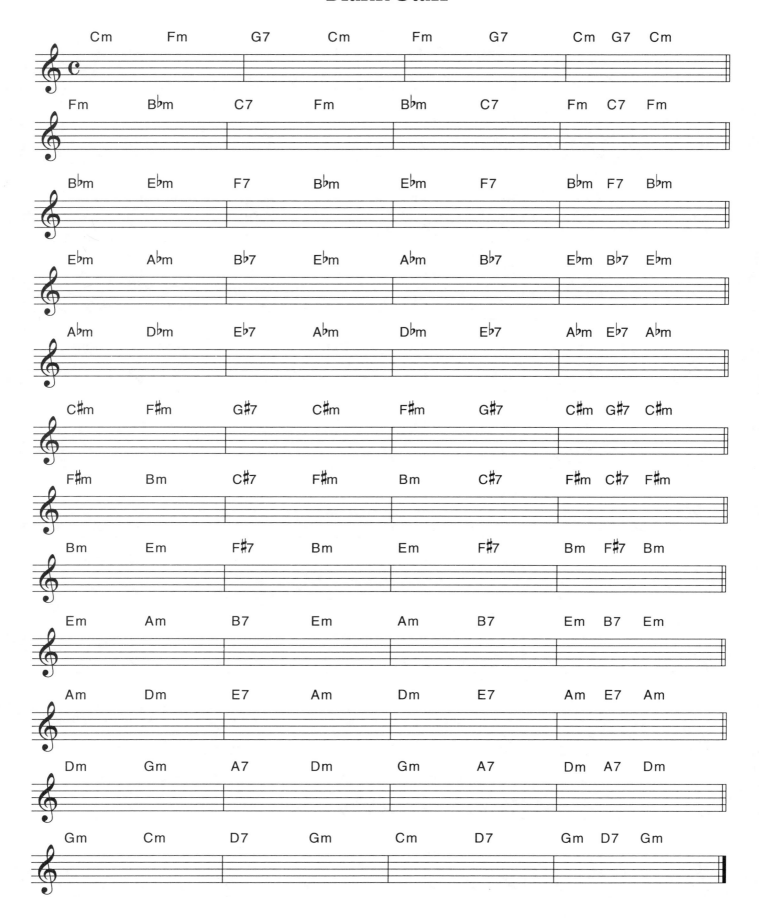

Chord and Bass Note

This chapter contains perhaps the most practical and useful way of using chords. Say for example, you want to sing a song while accompanying yourself on the piano. You can do this by playing the bass note in the left hand together with the chord in the right hand. This will give you a nice full sound on the piano. You can also experiment with moving the bass note down an octave which will give you an even richer sound.

2-5-1 Progression

In this chapter you will practice the chord over a so called 2-5-1 progression. This progression is very common in popular music. It's called 2-5-1 because the **first chord is based on the 2nd scale degree, the second chord is based on the 5th scale degree and the 3rd chord is based on the first scale degree.**

The layout of this chord progression is always the same:

FIRST CHORD (2-chord)-----------------Always minor
SECOND CHORD (5-chord)-------------Always Dominant 7
THIRD CHORD (1-chord)----------------Always Major

Scale degrees in the key of C Major

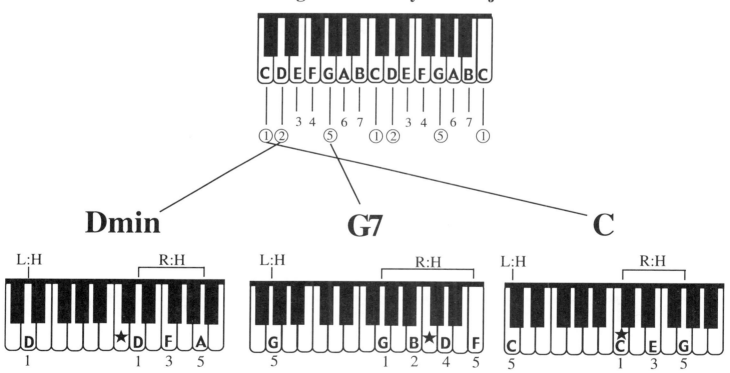

The following pages will help you get comfortable with the 2-5-1 progression. Each key has three different combinations of the inversions that you have already learned. Listen to the sound of the different combinations to get an idea of how many ways you can play an accompaniment.

C Major

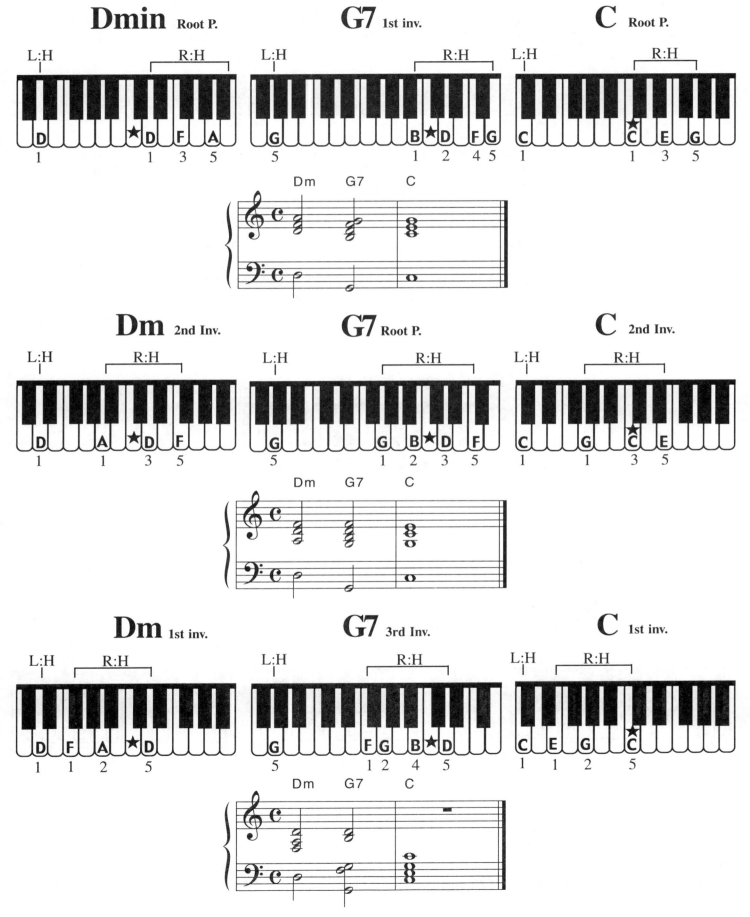

F Major

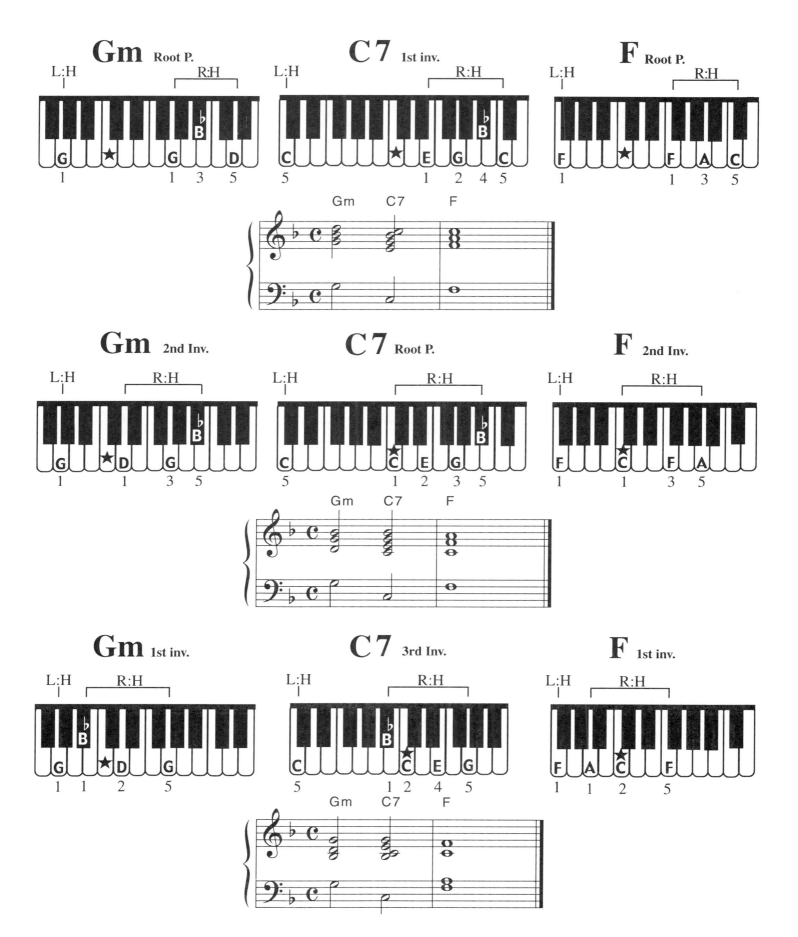

B♭ Major

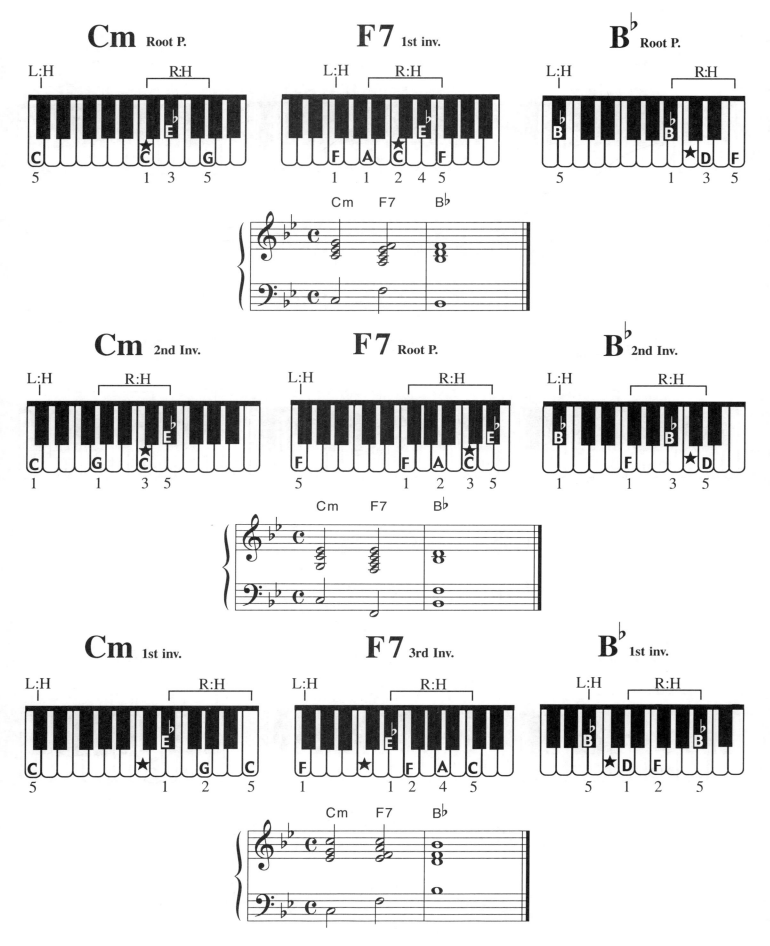

60

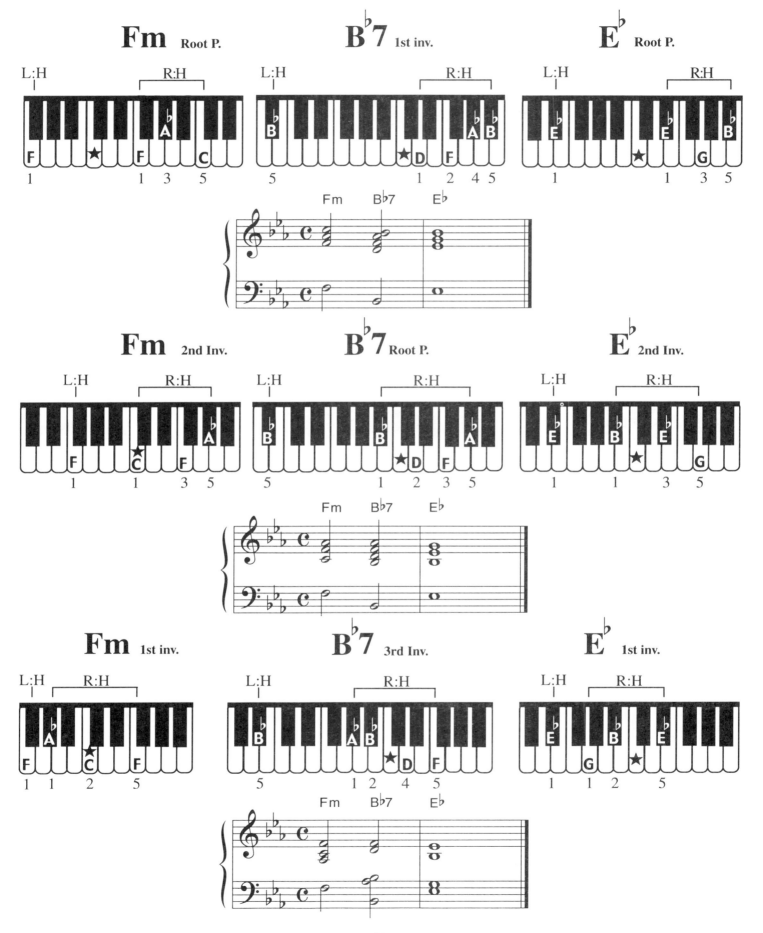

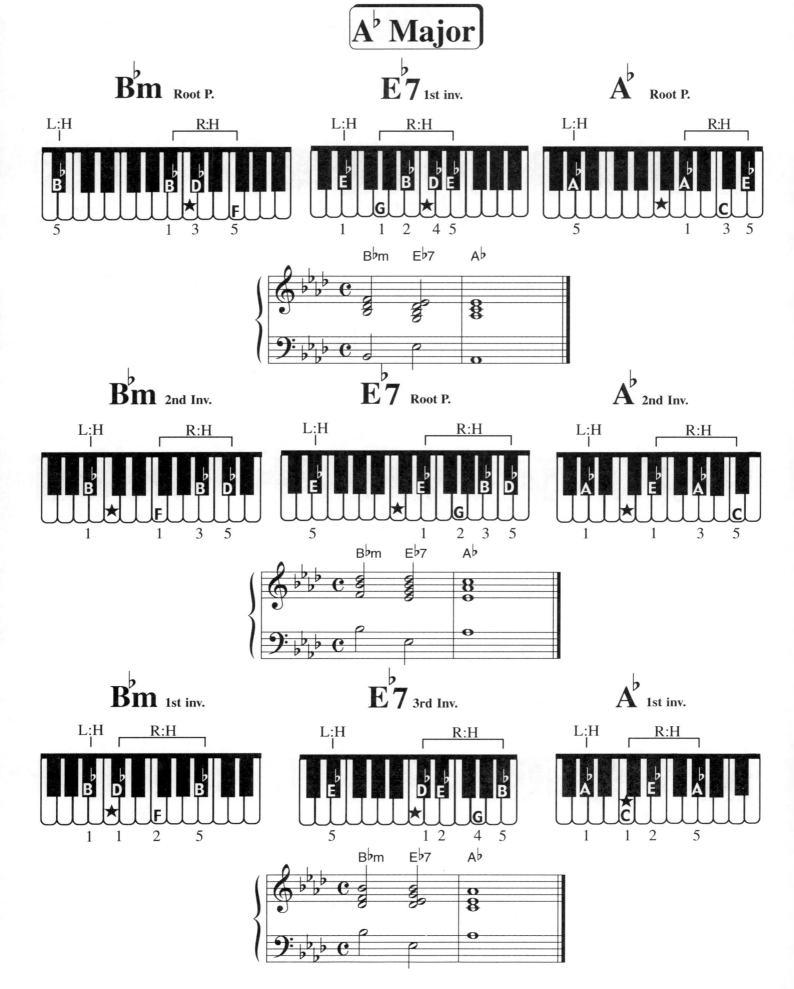

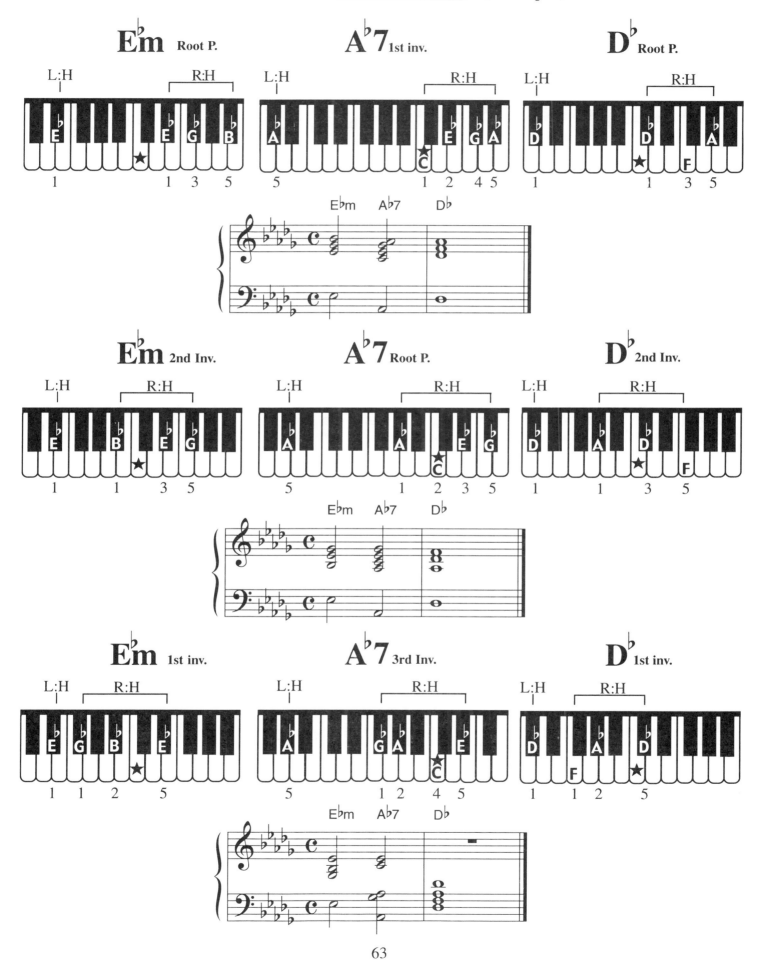

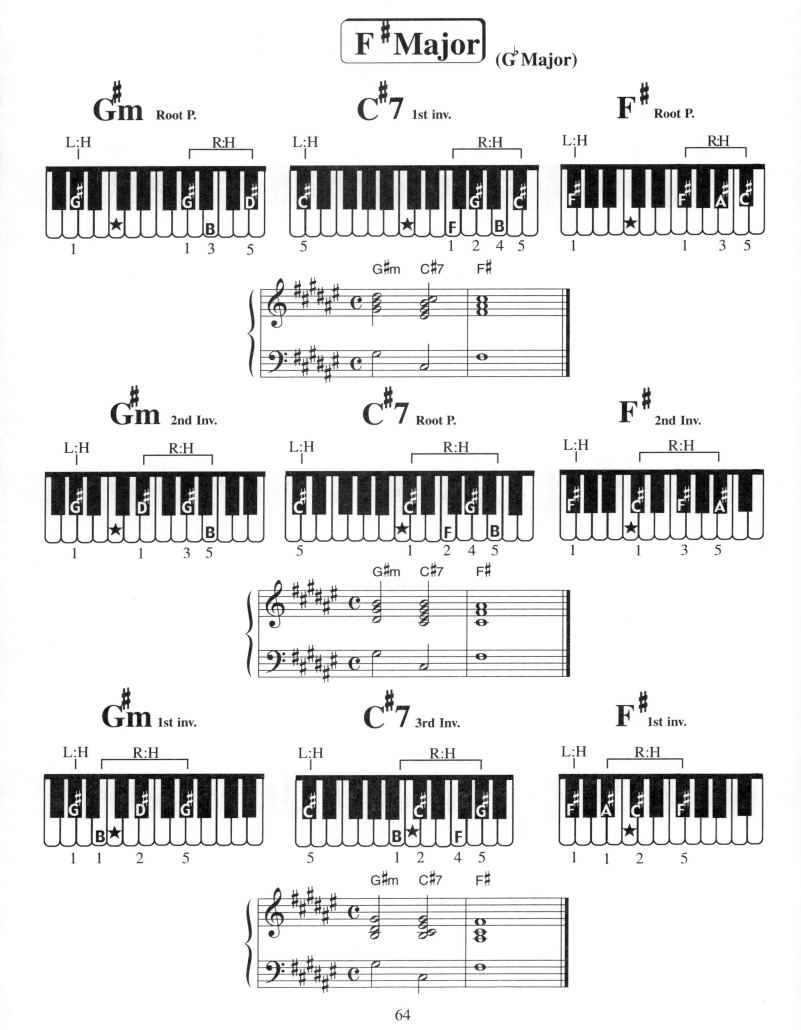

F# Major (G♭ Major)

64

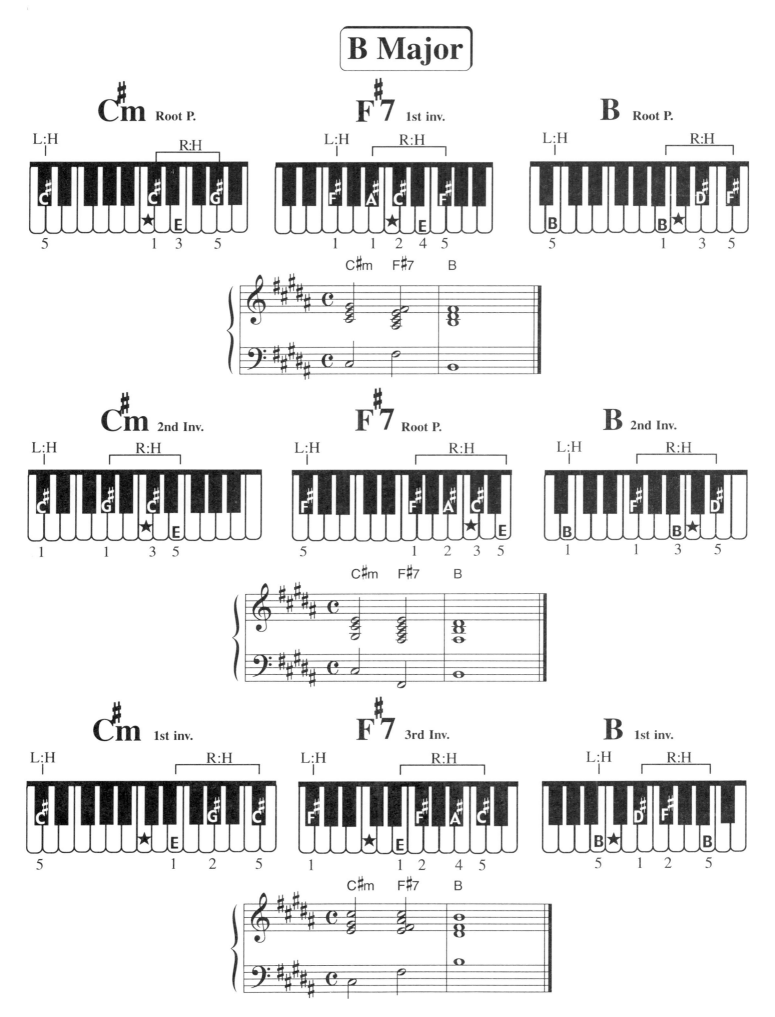

E Major

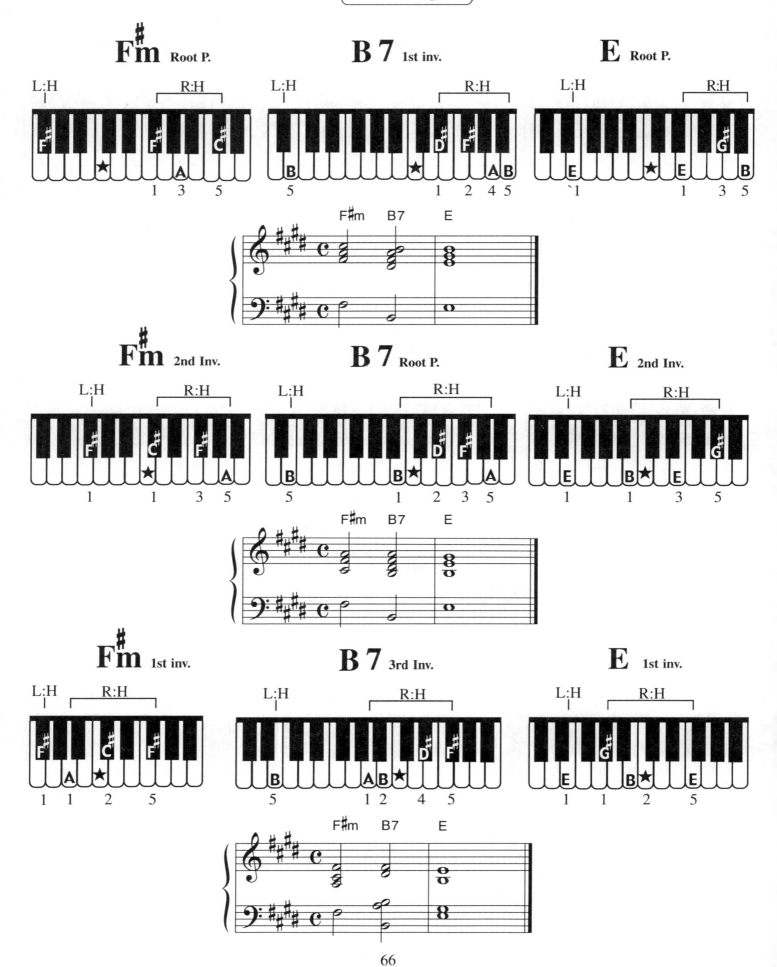

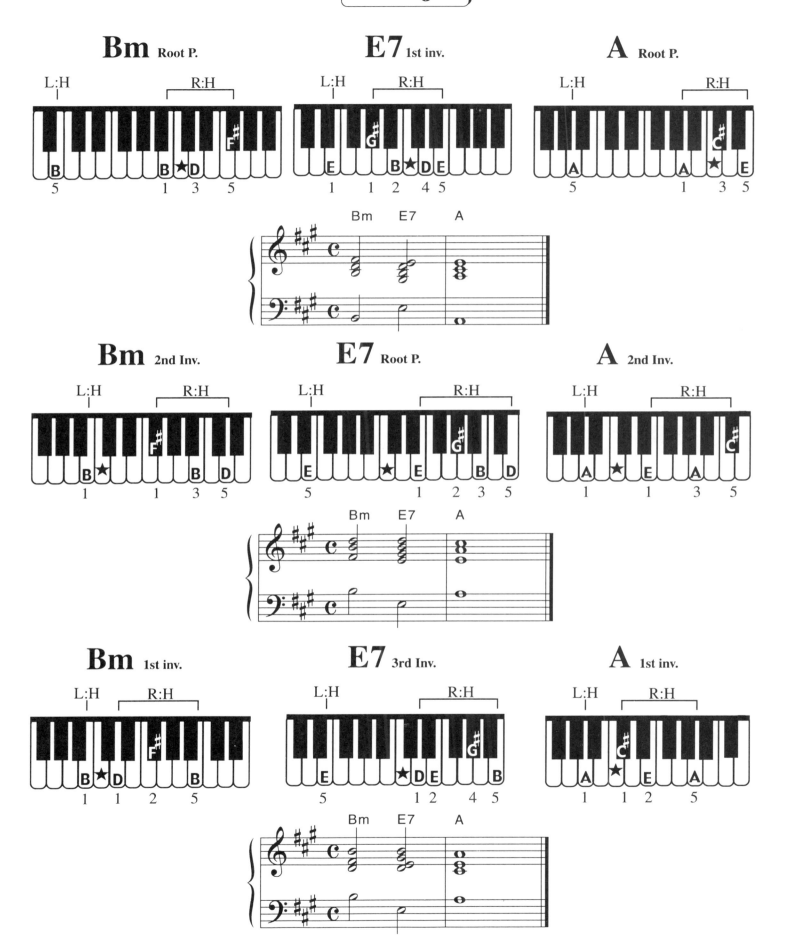

D Major

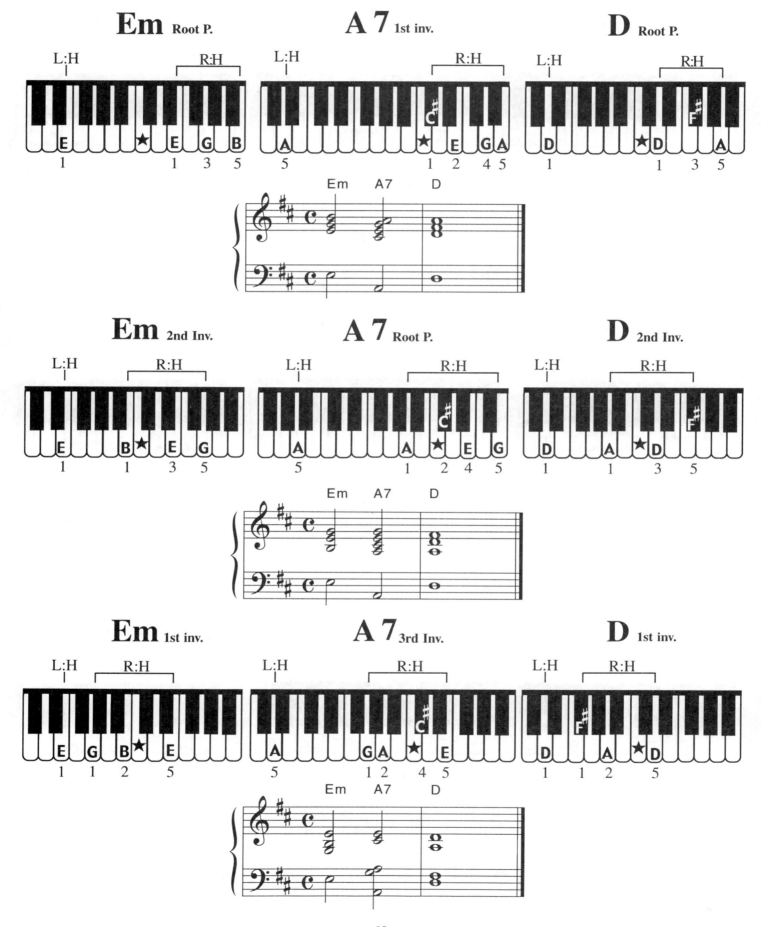

68

G Major

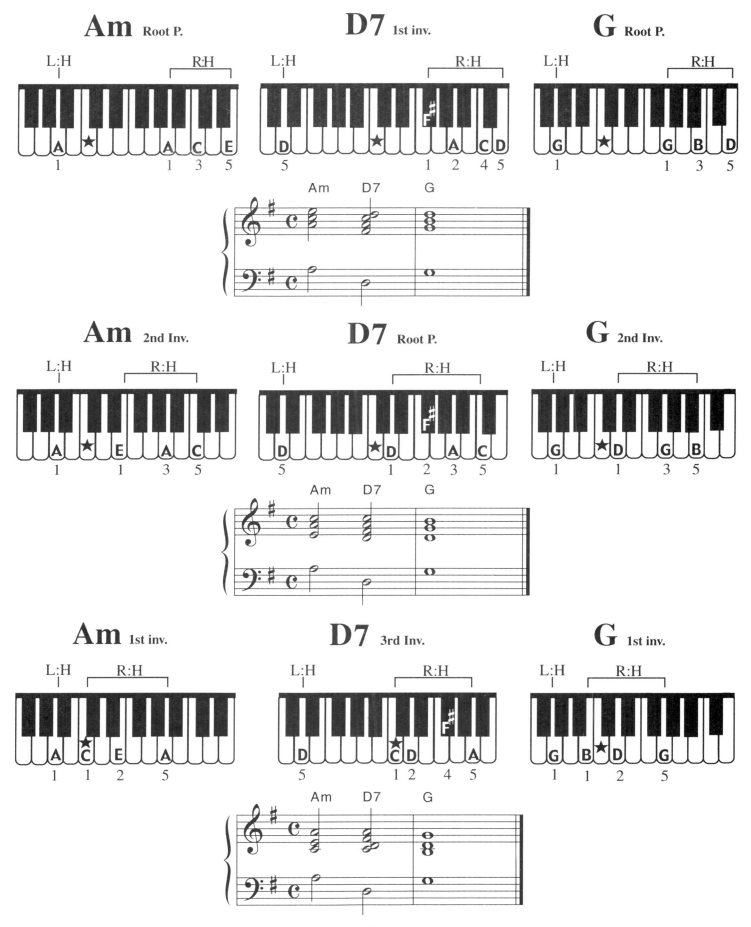

2-5-1 Progression

Blank Staff

Open Voicings

So far we have learned the chords in close position. In other words, the notes have been stacked in an orderly fashion in the right or left hand. Now it is time open up the voicings and the sound. This is done by dividing up the notes between the left and right hand. You will quickly notice a big difference in sound.

C Close position

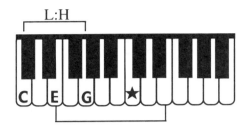

Move the E up an octave to create an open voicing.

C Open position

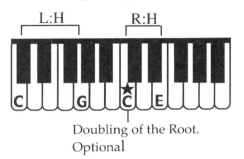

Doubling of the Root. Optional

G7 Close position

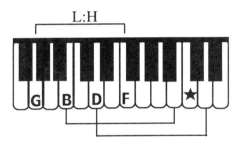

Move the B and D up an octave to create an open voicing.

G7 Open position

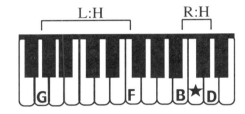

1-6-2-5 Progression

Just like the 2-5-1 progression, the 1-6-2-5 progression is very common in popular music. The quality of the chords may vary but the root movement stays the same. In the following examples the chord qualities are as follows:

FIRST CHORD -----------------Major Chord-----------First scale degree
SECOND CHORD--------------minor Chord-----------Sixth scale degree
THIRD CHORD-----------------minor Chord-----------Second scale degree
FOURTH CHORD--------------Dominant 7 Chord----Fifth scale degree

1-6-2-5 Progression in the key of C

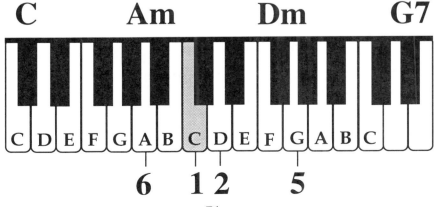

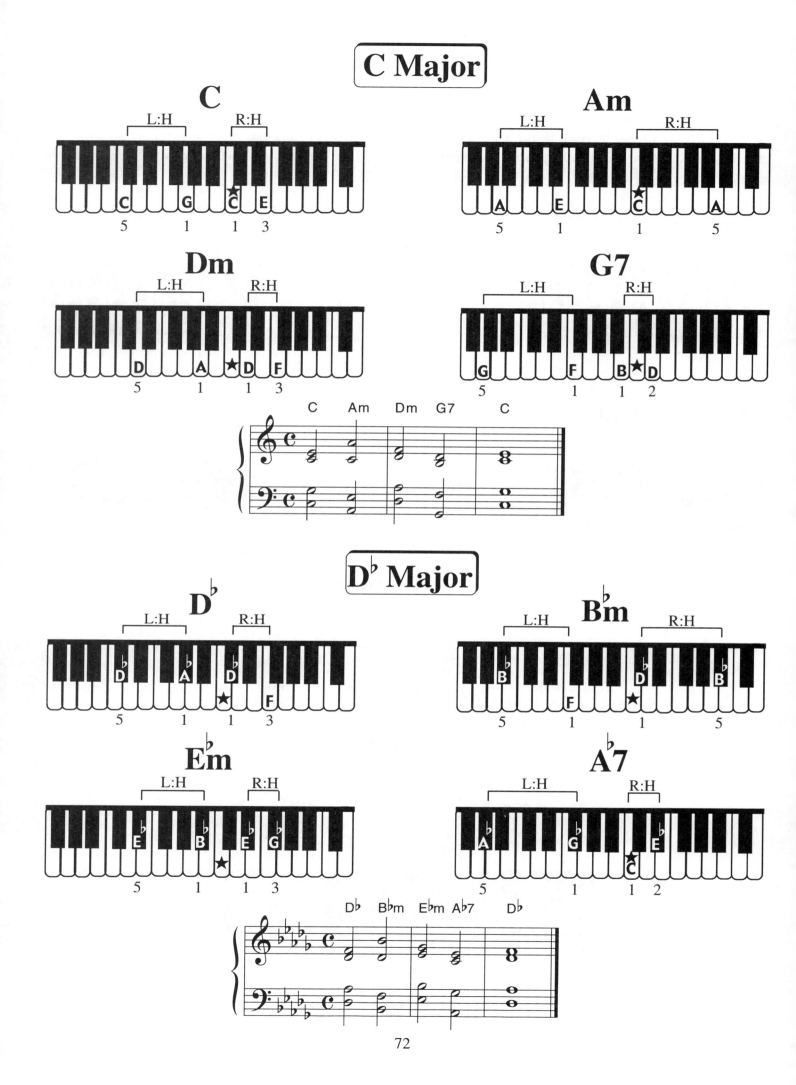

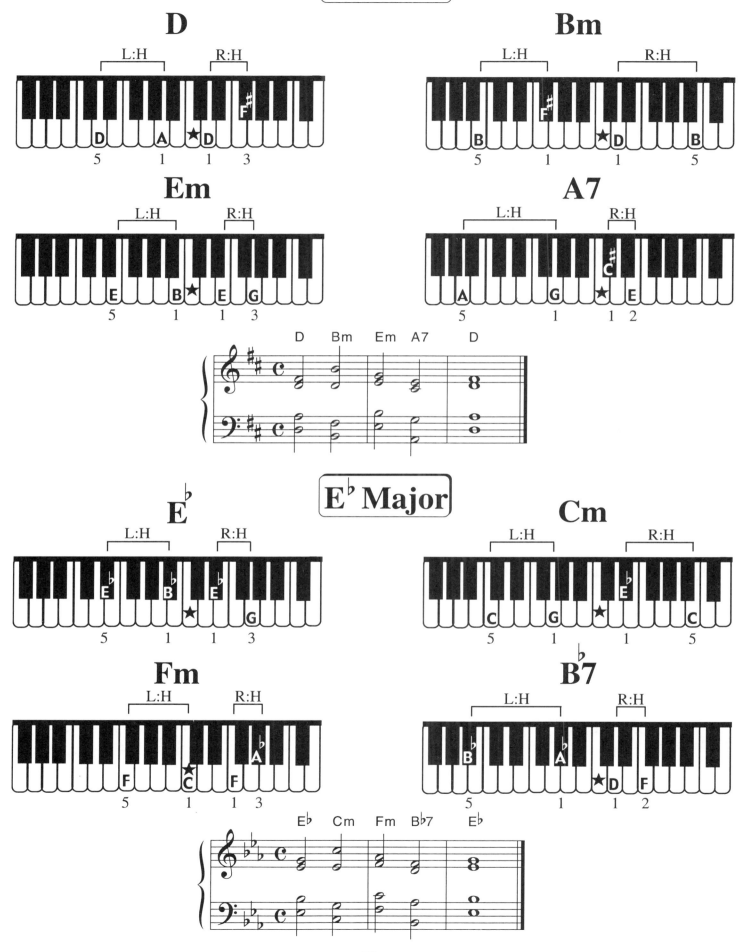

73

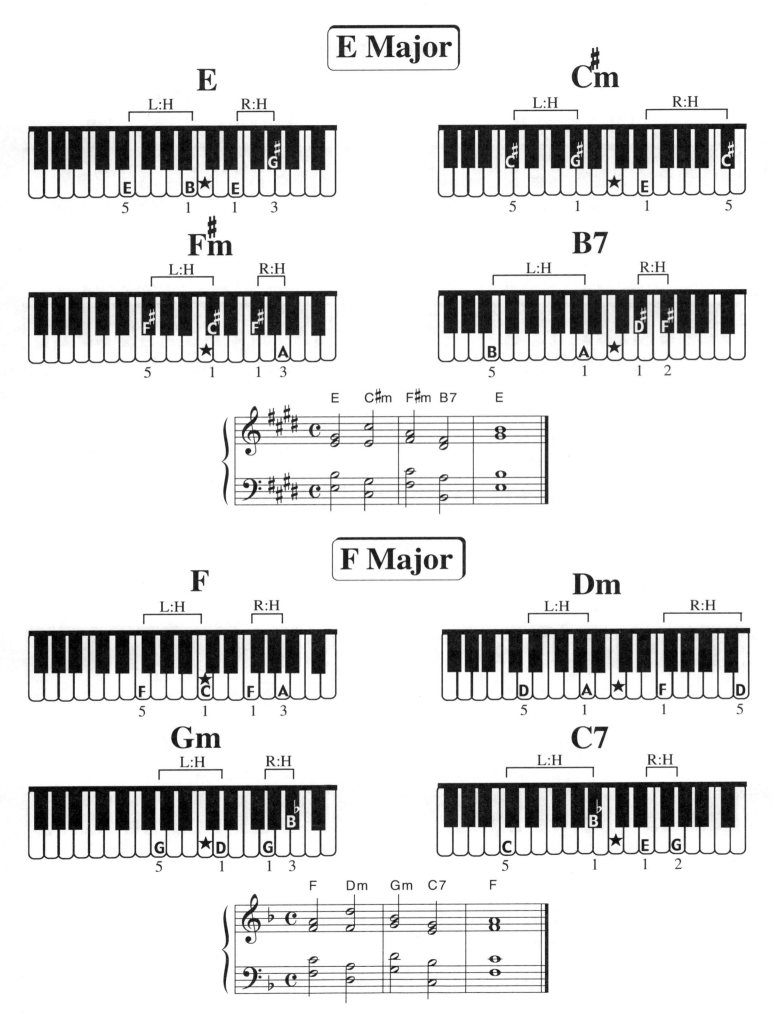

74

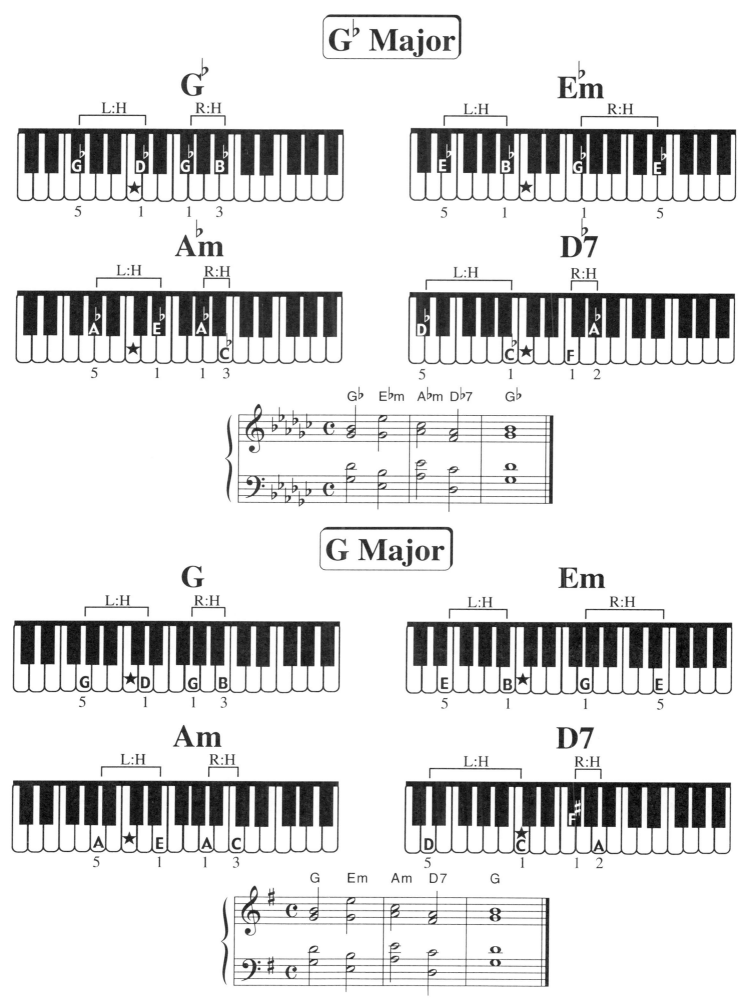

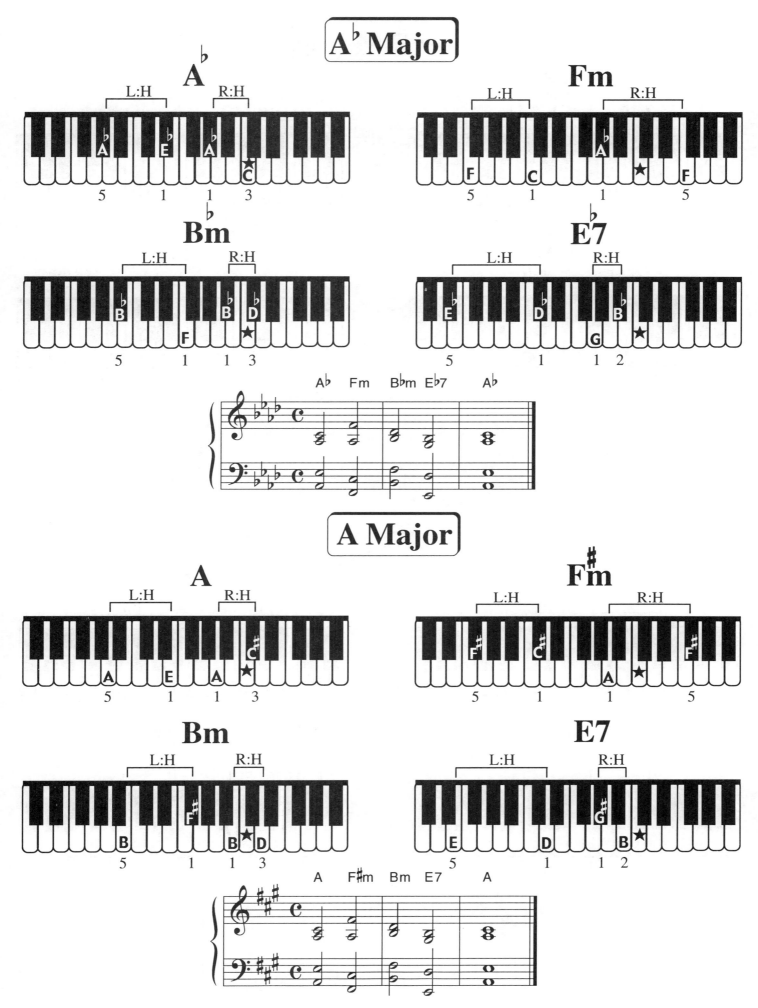

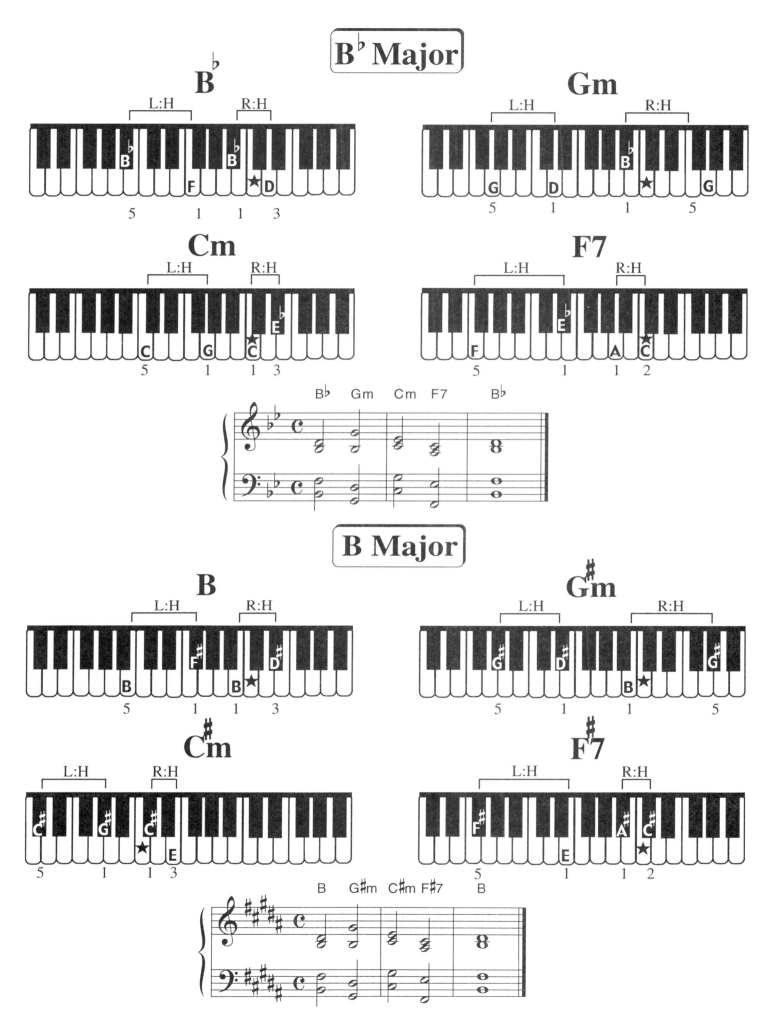

1-6-2-5 Progression

1-6-2-5 Progression
Blank Staff

More Open Voicings

The following section will introduce these chords:

Major 7th chords
minor 7th chords
Diminished 7th chords
Suspended chords
Augmented chords

When listening to skilled accompanists, you soon realize that they consistantly use open voicings and inversions. This is where the musicality and creativity plays an important part. In order to be creative you must be proficient and knowledgeable in the construction of chords. Remember that a soloist will sound much better with a good accompanist. Likewise, if you accompany yourself, your singing will sound better if you are comfortable with the chords and voicings.

I highly recommend devoting some time to this section of the book. When you've learned to combine the chords in the following section with the chords you've already learned, your playing will reach a higher level.

Major 7th Chords

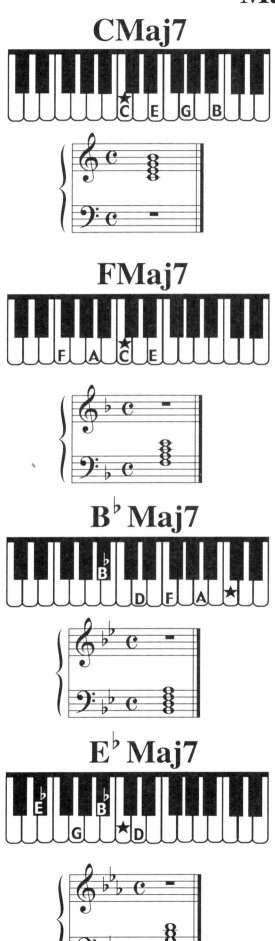
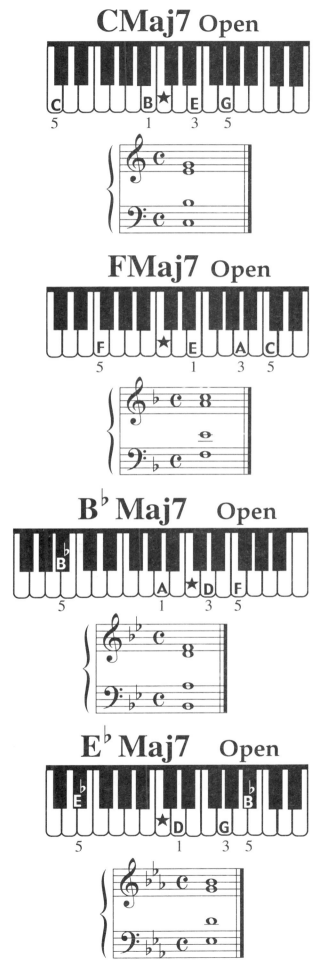

81

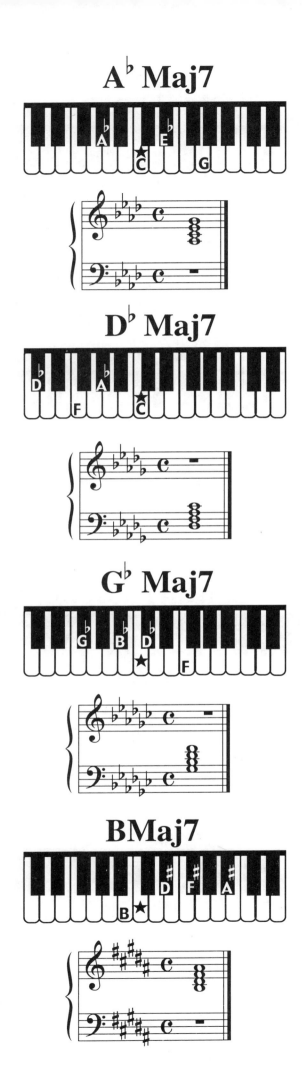
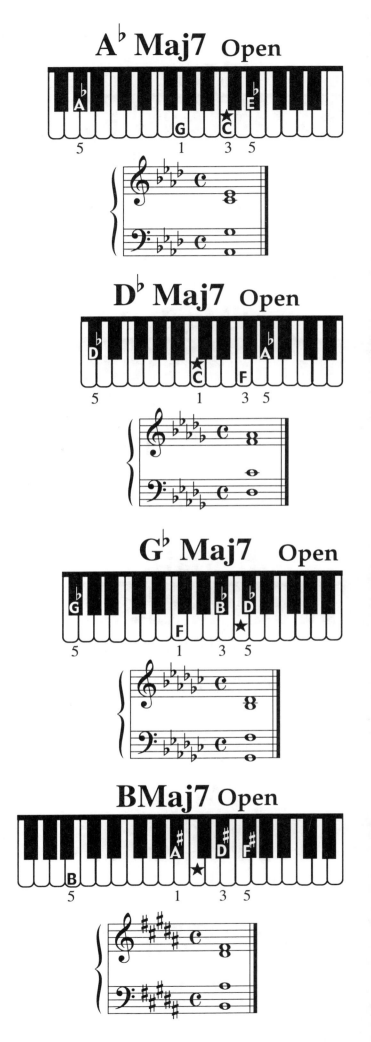

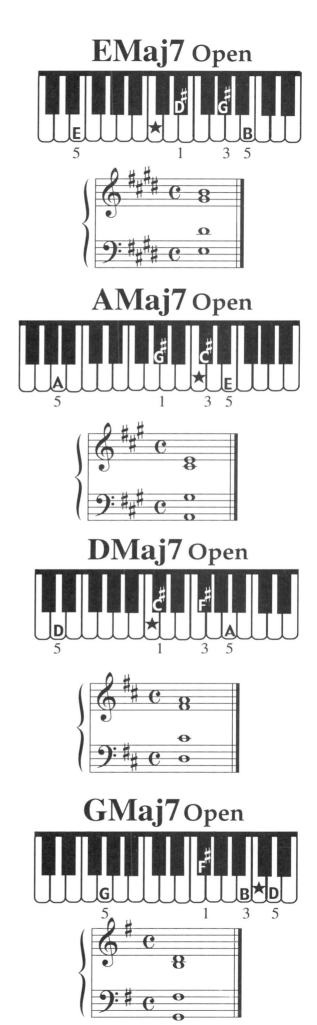

Minor 7th Chords

Note that there are no key signature indicated. Each chord is shown with accidentals.
The reason is that the min7th chord can have several different harmonic functions.

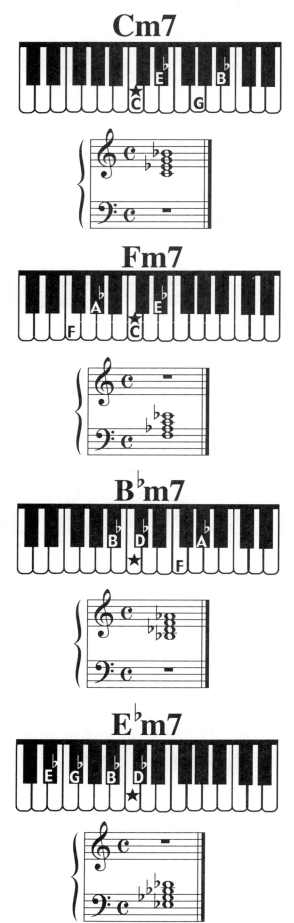

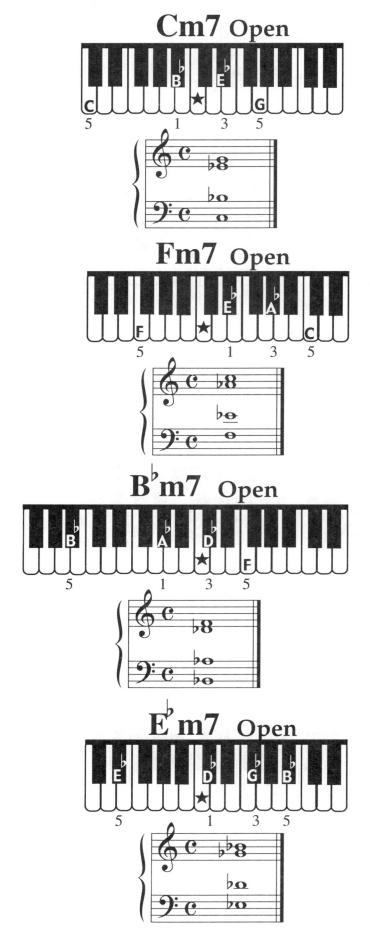

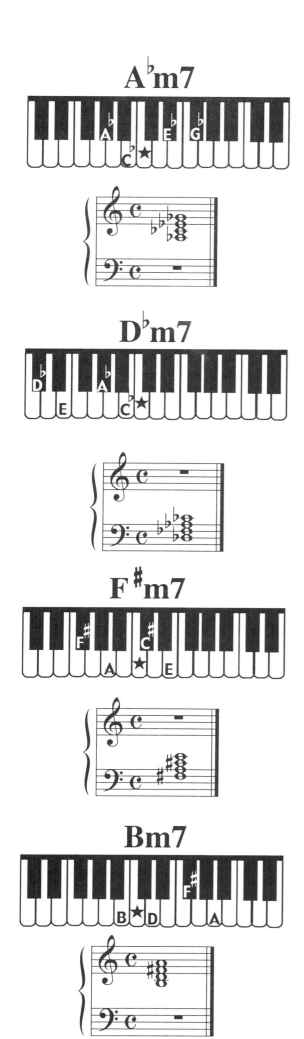

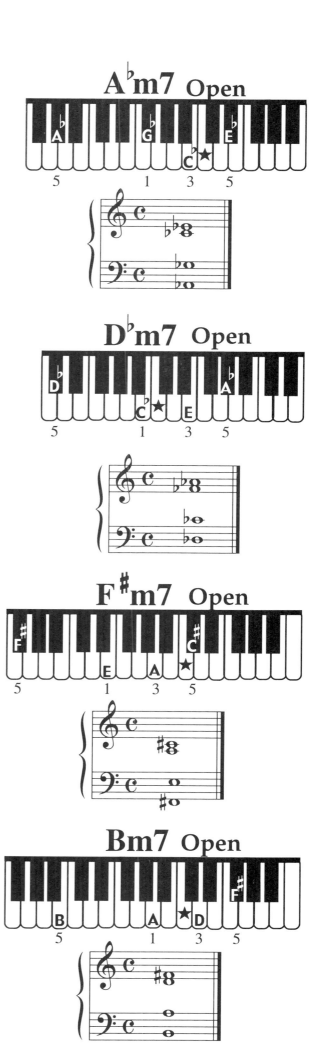

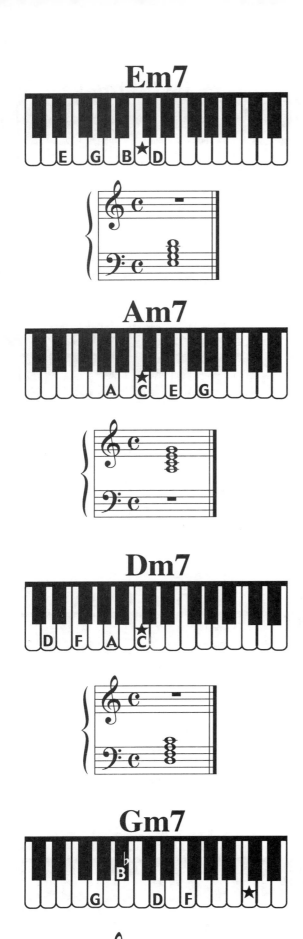
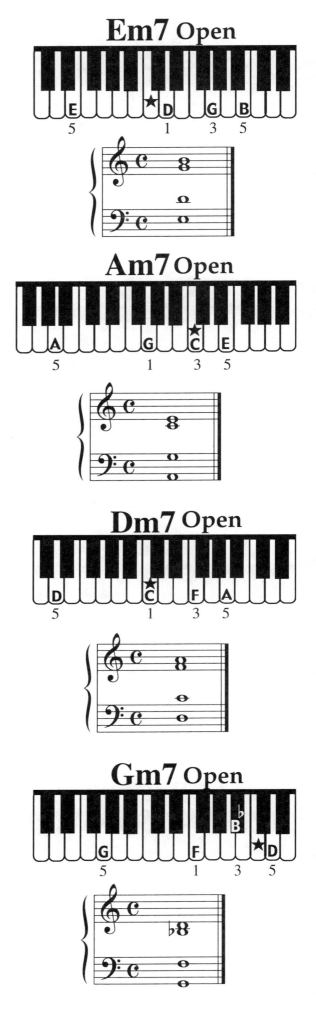

Diminished 7th chords

Diminished 7th chords are perhaps the easiest chords to learn and remember. The reason is because they are constructed in a symmetrical fashion by stacking minor thirds (see appendix about minor thirds and other intervals). As a result, there are only 3 different combinations that make up all twelve diminished 7th chords. The diagrams below show you these three different combinations.

Gdim7

B♭dim7

D♭dim7/C#dim

Edim7

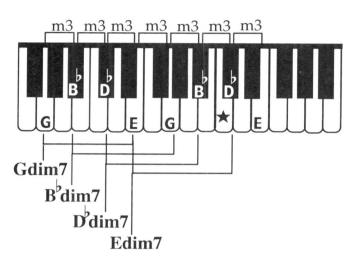

A♭dim7/G#dim

Bdim7

Ddim7

Fdim7

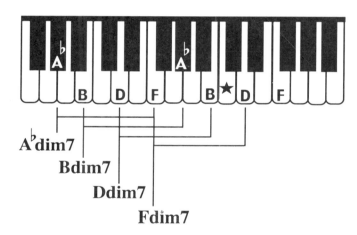

Adim7

Cdim7

D#dim/E♭dim7

F#dim/G♭dim7

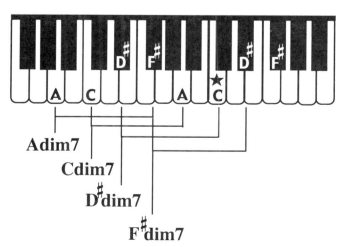

Note: A diminished chord is also indicated by a circle after the name of the chord.

Cᵒ = Cdim

87

Diminished 7th chords

Cdim7

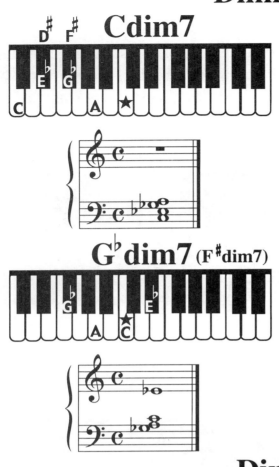

E♭dim7

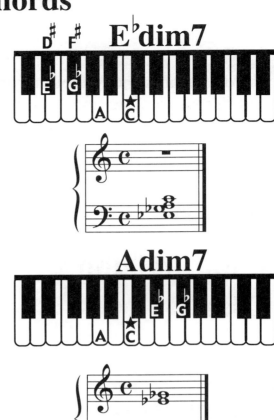

G♭dim7 (F♯dim7)

Adim7

Dim7 Open Voicing

Cdim7

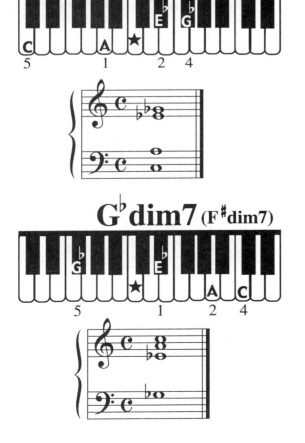

E♭dim7

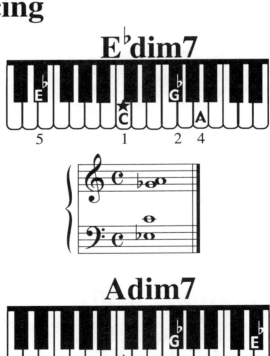

G♭dim7 (F♯dim7)

Adim7

Diminished 7th chords

C#dim7 (D♭dim7)

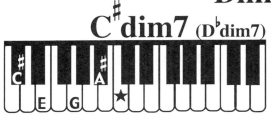

Edim7

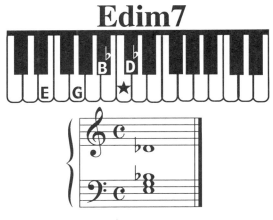

Gdim7

B♭dim7

Dim7 Open Voicing

C#dim7 (D♭dim7)

Edim7

Gdim7

B♭dim7

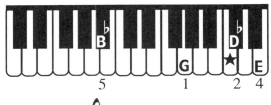

Diminished 7th chords

Ddim7

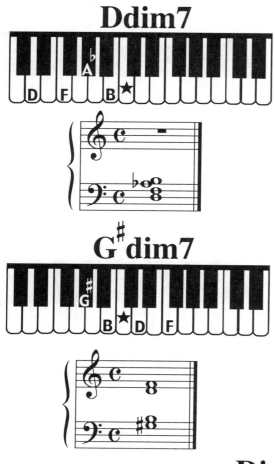

Fdim7

G#dim7

Bdim7

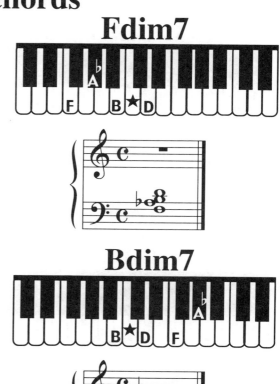

Dim7 Open Voicing

Ddim7

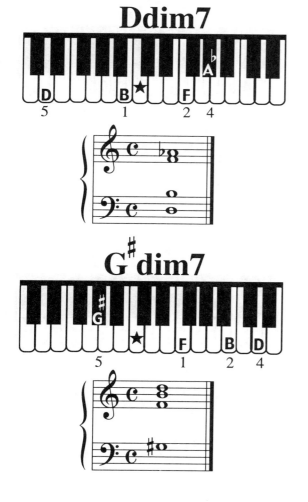

Fdim7

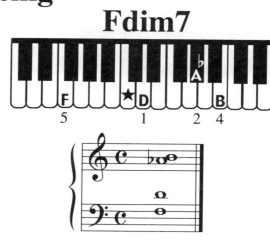

G#dim7

Bdim7

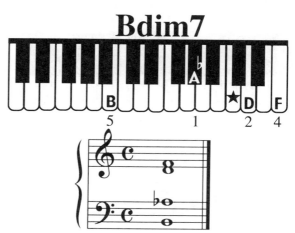

90

Augmented/Suspended Chords

In popular music, suspended and augmented chords are often used in a dominant fashion. In other words, it's common to replace a C7 with an augmented C chord or a suspended C chord. Listen carefully to the tension in the sound of these chords and their strong urge to resolve to the tonic.

Augmented Chords:

An augmented chord is created by raising the fifth a half step. If the chord has a dominant function, it can be strengthened by adding the dominant (lowered) seventh. The Augmented 7th chord sounds great in an open voicing.

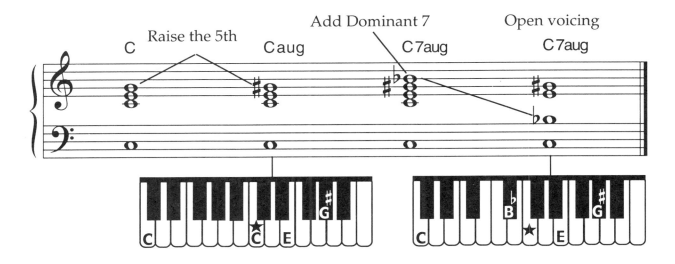

Suspended Chords:

A suspended chord is created by raising the third a half step. Another way to look at it is to replace the 3rd scale degree with the 4th scale degree. If the chord has a dominant function, strenghten it by adding the dominant seventh. Listen carefully to the sound of the suspended chord. You'll notice that it has a smoother sound than the augmented chord, especially when played in an open voicing.

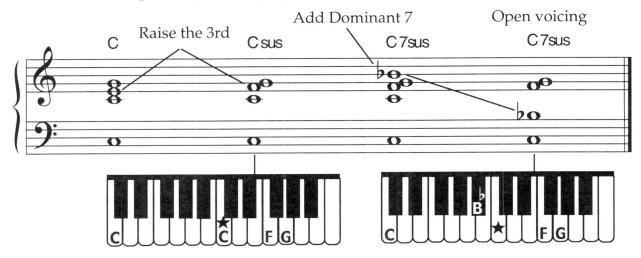

Augmented Chords

Caug
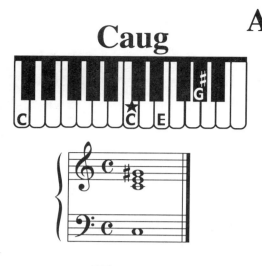

C7aug
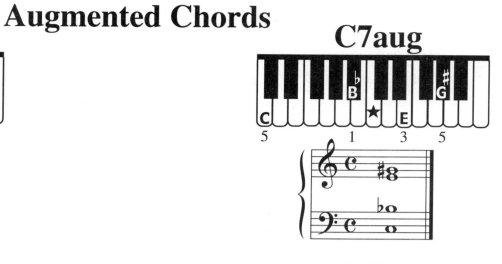

Faug

F7aug
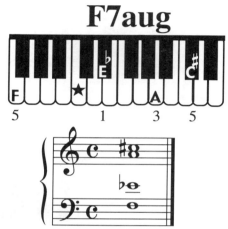

B♭aug

B♭7aug

E♭aug

E♭7aug
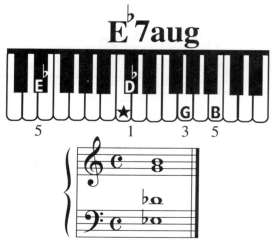

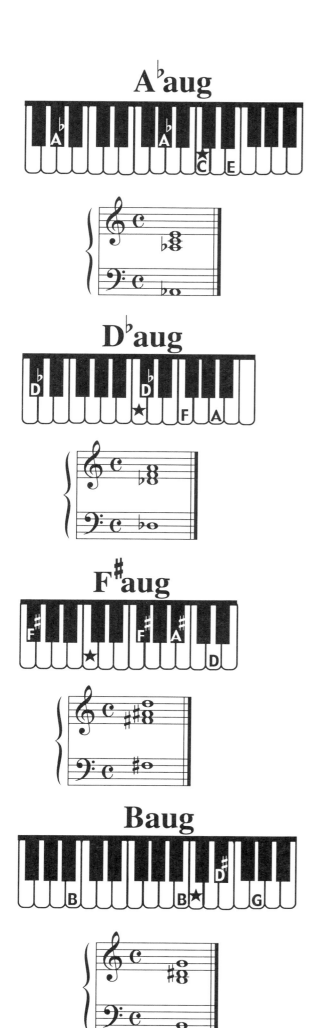

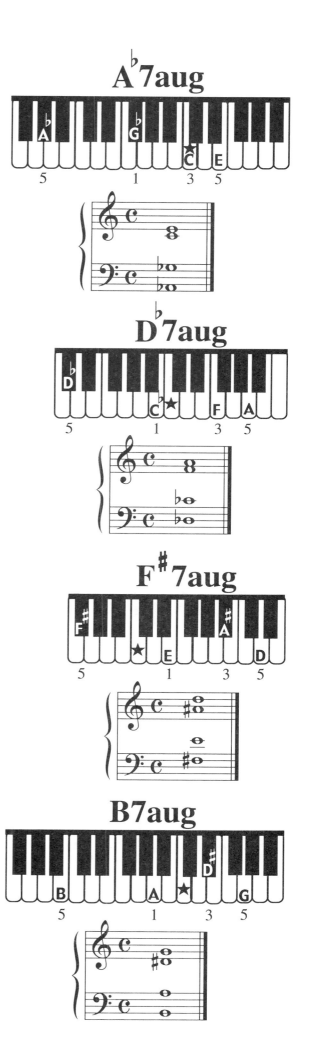

Eaug

E7aug

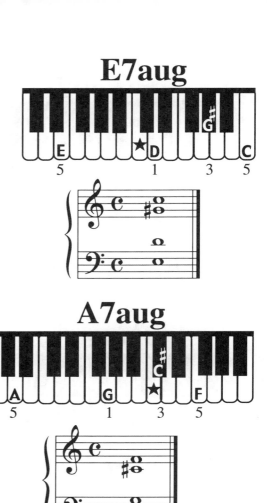

Aaug

A7aug

Daug

D7aug

Gaug

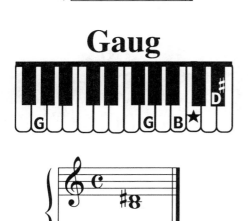

G7aug

Augmented Progression

The augmented chord often functions as a dominant chord. The following progression will help you become familiar with this common harmonic movement.

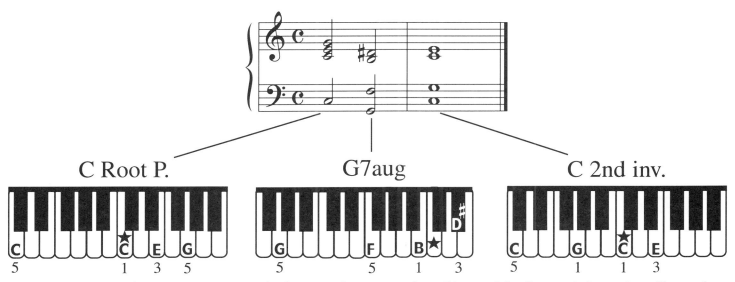

Practice the progressions below to become familiar with the voicings in all twelve keys. You can use the previous chapters as a reference to find the chord voicings.

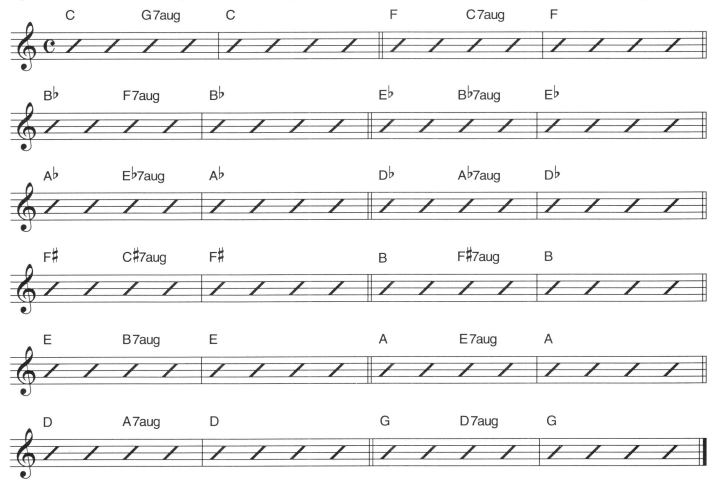

Note: The indicated voicings on this page are only one way of playing the progressions. You should experiment with different inversions to make the chords fit the song.

Suspended Chords

Csus
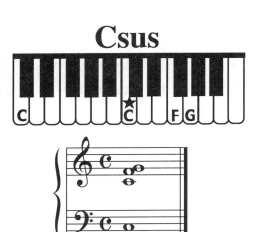

C7sus
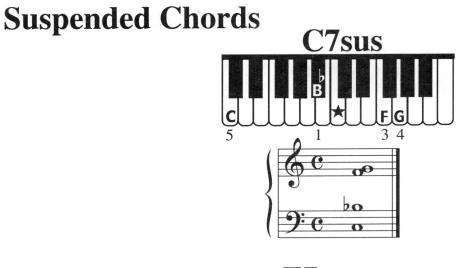

Fsus
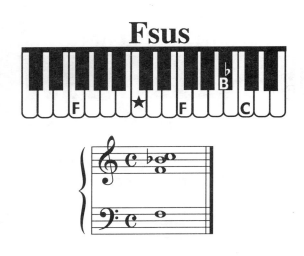

F7sus
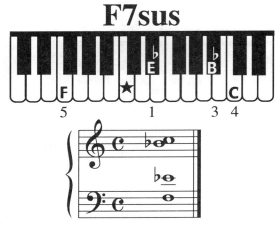

B♭sus
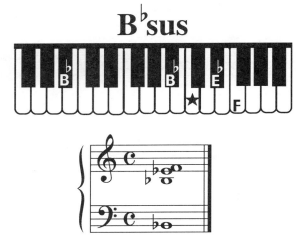

B♭7sus
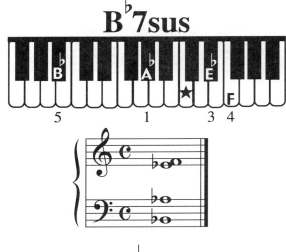

E♭sus
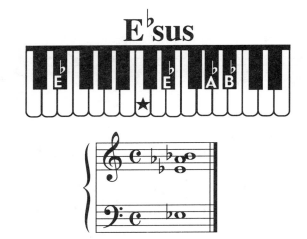

E♭7sus
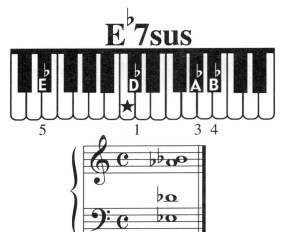

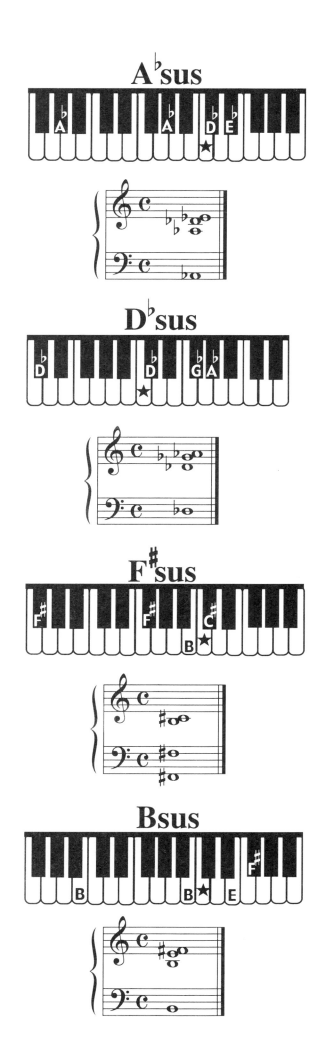

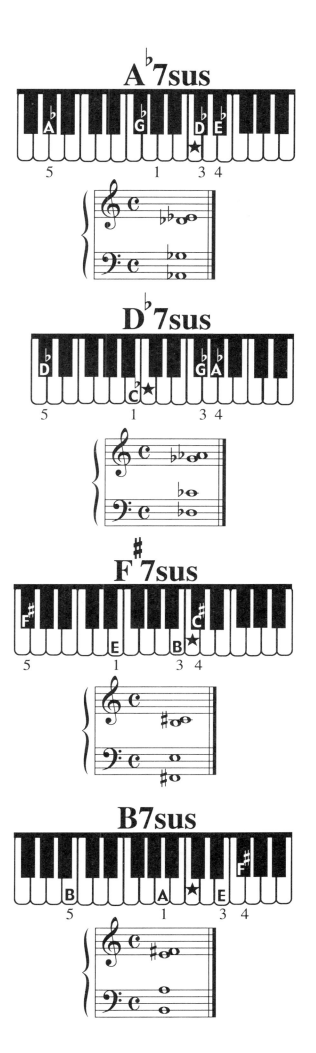

Esus

E7sus

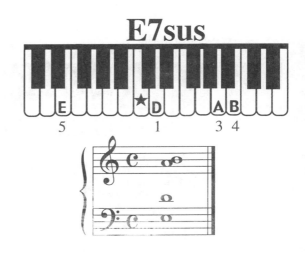

Asus

A7sus

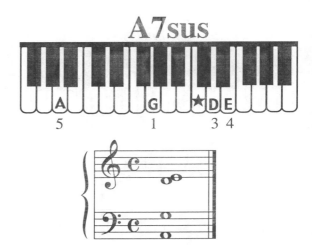

Dsus

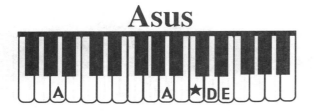

D7sus

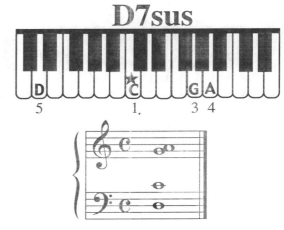

Gsus

G7sus

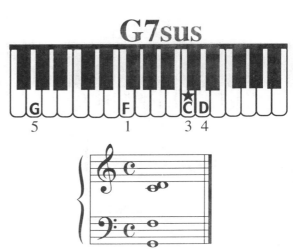

Suspended Progression

Much like the augmented chord, the suspended chord often functions as a dominant chord. Learn the progression below and try to play it in all twelve keys.

Note: The voicings indicated on this page are only one way of playing the progression. You should experiment with different inversions to make the chords fit the song.

Alternate Bass Note

When reading the sheet music of your favorite songs, you will most likely come across chords that include an alternate bass note. This method it often used to create a smoother bass line and to alter the sound of a chord. The sound of the chords you have learned so far can be changed by simply playing a different bass note. Experiment with changing the bass note of the chords you already know. You'll be amazed by all the new sounds.

This is how it works:
The letter to the left of the slash indicates the chord.
The letter to the right of the slash indicates the bass note

Chord — C/E — Bass Note

Play and listen to the sound of these chords.

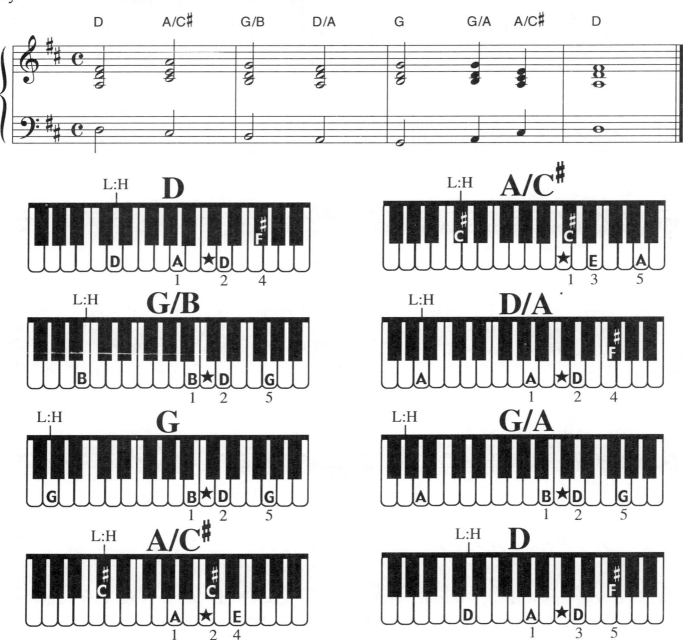

Alternate Bass Note Progressions

Here are some examples of chord progressions using alternate bass notes. Listen carefully to the sound of these chords. Experiment with making up your own combinations and write down the ones you like. Blank music paper is provided in the back of the book.

Adding the 9th

The world of harmony ranges from simple triads to complex combinations of notes in different intervals. Without diving too deeply into music theory, adding the 9th scale degree is a great way of creating a rich new sound to the chords that you've already learned.

This is how it works:
In the key of C, count 9 notes from C and you'll end up on a D.

Think of it like this. The 9th is the note a **whole step** above the chord name.

Chord		**9th**
C	————	D
F7	————	G
B♭	————	C
Em	————	F♯

Because of the relationship between the chord name and the 9th, you'll sometimes see a chord symbol with the number 2 included, C2 for example. That means to add the second scale degree, which in a C chord would be the note D (same as the 9th).

When the 9th is included in the chord symbol you should add it. When it is not, it becomes a judgement call. You can choose to play it or leave it out. Do whatever sounds best to you. Generally, the 9th creates a thicker texture and adds more tension to the sound.

Cadd9	————————	C triad	——	add D
CMaj9	————————	C Maj7	——	add D
Cmin9	————————	C minor 7	——	add D
C9	————————	C7	——	add D
Csus9	————————	C7sus	——	add D

The keyboard diagrams below show you how to add the 9th. When the 9th is added you don't have to play the root of the chord in the right hand, especially if you're already playing it in the left hand.

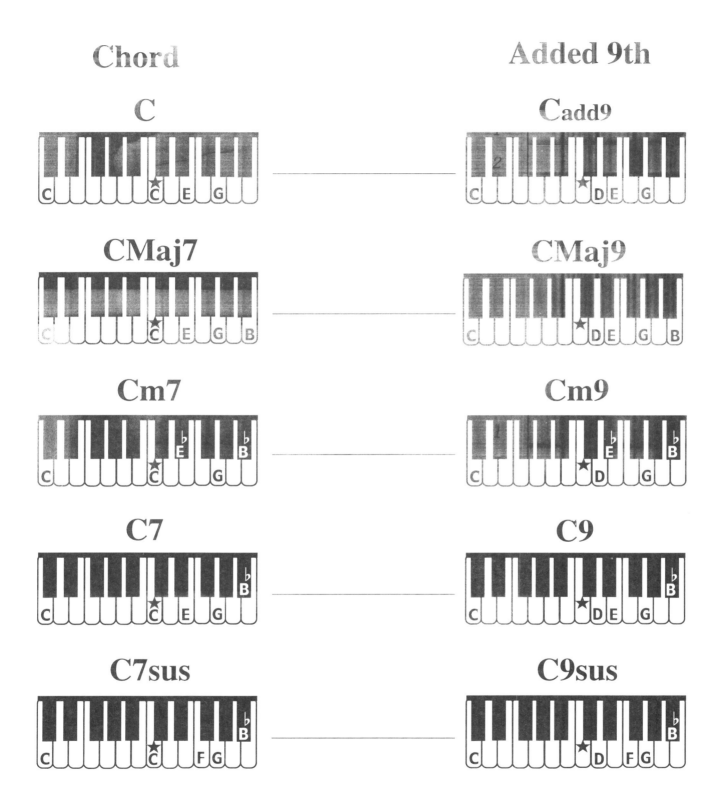

Chord   **Added 9th**

C   Cadd9

CMaj7   CMaj9

Cm7   Cm9

C7   C9

C7sus   C9sus

Experiment with adding the 9th. Keep in mind that any chord you play can be played in inversions, including chords with an added 9th. The combinations are endless, which you will notice as you become more familiar with playing piano chords.

Appendix

This section serves as an introduction to music theory. Its purpose is to introduce you to some basic theory, which will be helpful when learning chords. The more familiar you are with note names, keys, scales, intervals etc., the easier it will be to use chords to accompany yourself or someone else. Remember to use your ears and listen carefully to everything you play. In doing this, you'll become your own teacher and will discover that *You Can Teach Yourself Piano Chords*.

The Keyboard

The keyboard is a symmetrical combination of white and black keys. Because of its logical layout it is one of the easiest instruments to actually **see** notes and chords. In this book we use a visual method to help you learn to play the combinations of notes we call chords.

This layout is the same for all keyboards and will never change. Therefore, once you remember the distance from one note to another, or how it feels when you play a chord, you will have learned it for the rest of your life.

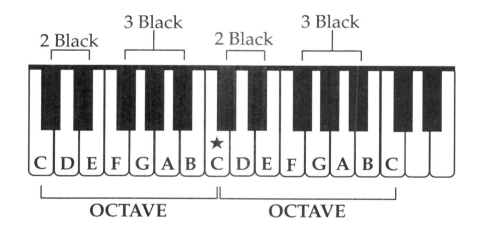

The distance from a note to the next note with the same name is called an **OCTAVE**. A melody or a chord can be played in different octaves. When you experiment with this you will soon find out in which octave it sounds the best. If you play a chord too low it will sound muddy, and if too high it will sound thin.

In this book the chords are positioned in relation to Middle C. Find Middle C on your keyboard. It is located in the middle of the keyboard by the key hole (if you have a piano that you can lock). Some electronic keyboards have middle C indicated. The technical location of Middle C is a sixth below A 440, so if you are into physics it should be easy to find. **Middle C is indicated with a star ★ in all the illustrations in this book.**

Musical Alphabet

There are seven letters in the music alphabet.
They are the same as the regular alphabet.

$$\boxed{A \ B \ C \ D \ E \ F \ G}$$

Any of the notes can be raised or lowered by a half step. A half step is the very next note, up or down, black or white.

$\boxed{\text{To } \textbf{raise} \text{ a note we use a sharp sign } \sharp}$

$\boxed{\text{To } \textbf{lower} \text{ a note we use a flat sign } \flat}$

The sharp sign $\sharp$, and the flat sign $\flat$, are called **accidentals**.

For example: The note **D** can be moved up or down to become $D^\sharp$ or $D^\flat$. If you look at the diagram below you'll notice that $D\sharp$ is the same note as $E\flat$, and $D\flat$ is the same note as $C\sharp$. When the same note has two different names, they are called **enharmonic** notes.

FLAT NOTES $\flat$

SHARP NOTES $\sharp$

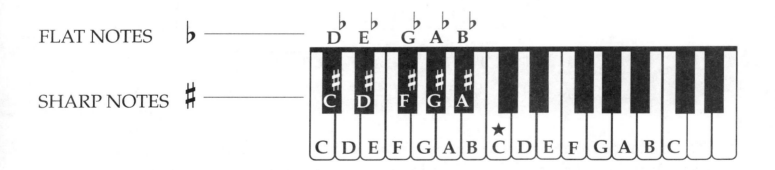

More examples of enharmonic notes:

$$E\sharp = F$$
$$B\sharp = C$$
$$F\flat = E$$
$$C\flat = B$$

106

The Grand Staff

Treble Clef — Played by the Right hand.

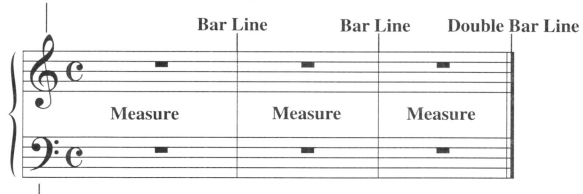

Bass Clef — Played by the Left hand.

Note

A note has a stem and a note head.

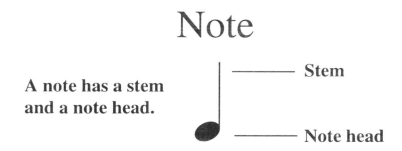

Notes are written on the lines or in the spaces.

Notation

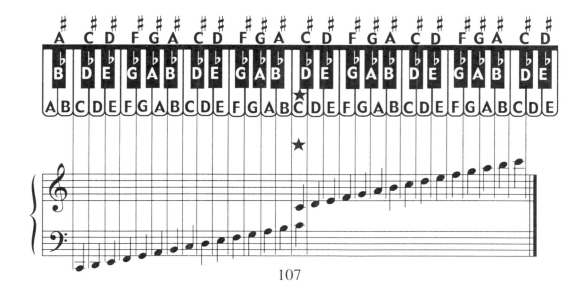

Keys/Scales

Each half step in the scale has its own corresponding key. Since there are 12 half steps there are twelve keys, major and minor. Any melody or chord progression that you learn can be played in another key. Changing keys is called **transposing**. Each key is determined by the number of accidentals (sharps and flats).

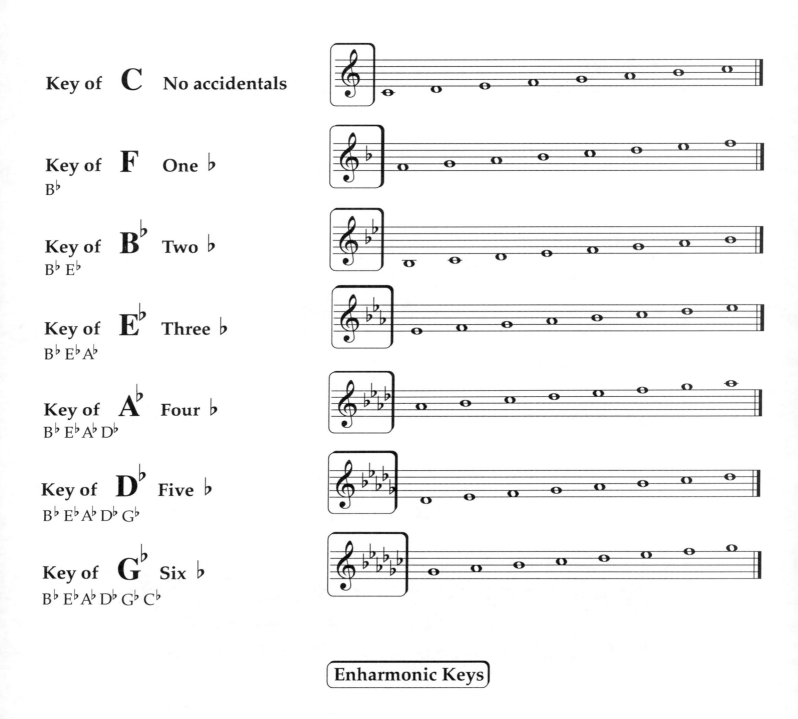

Key of **C** No accidentals

Key of **F** One ♭
B♭

Key of **B♭** Two ♭
B♭ E♭

Key of **E♭** Three ♭
B♭ E♭ A♭

Key of **A♭** Four ♭
B♭ E♭ A♭ D♭

Key of **D♭** Five ♭
B♭ E♭ A♭ D♭ G♭

Key of **G♭** Six ♭
B♭ E♭ A♭ D♭ G♭ C♭

Enharmonic Keys

Enharmonic keys are keys that have the same notes but different accidentals.
On the next page you will notice: 1. C♯ has the same notes as D♭.
                                    2. F♯ has the same notes as G♭.

Key of **C♯** Seven ♯
F♯ C♯ G♯ D♯ A♯ E♯ B♯

Key of **F♯** Six ♯
F♯ C♯ G♯ D♯ A♯ E♯

Key of **B** Five ♯
F♯ C♯ G♯ D♯ A♯

Key of **E** Four ♯
F♯ C♯ G♯ D♯

Key of **A** Three ♯
F♯ C♯ G♯

Key of **D** Two ♯
F♯ C♯

Key of **G** One ♯
F♯

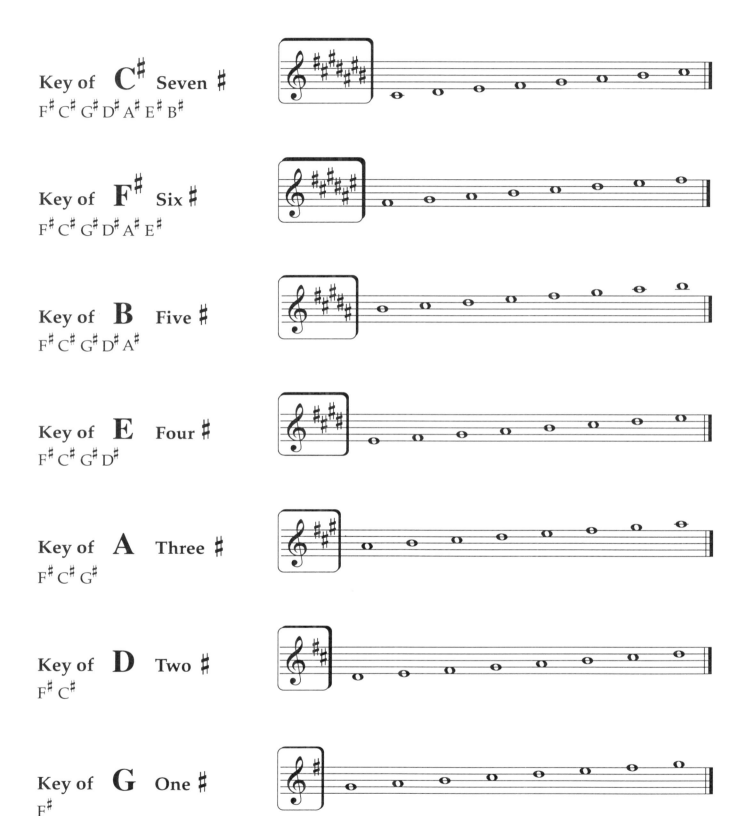

Scale Degrees/Diatonic Chords

A chord can be built on any note in a scale. Chords that move up and down a given scale are called **diatonic chords**. Following is an example of how diatonic triads work over a C major scale and what qualities they have.

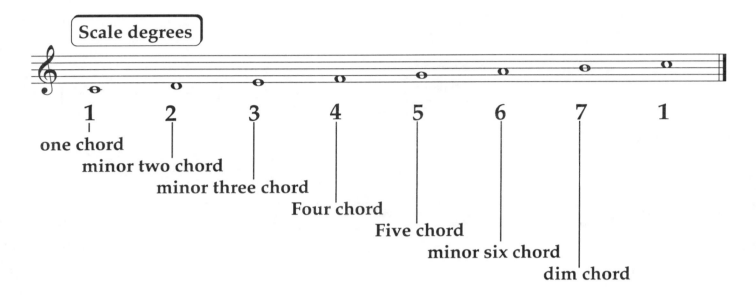

The first chords that are taught in standard music theory are the **tonic, sub-dominant and dominant chords**. They are harmonically very strong and play an important part in western music.

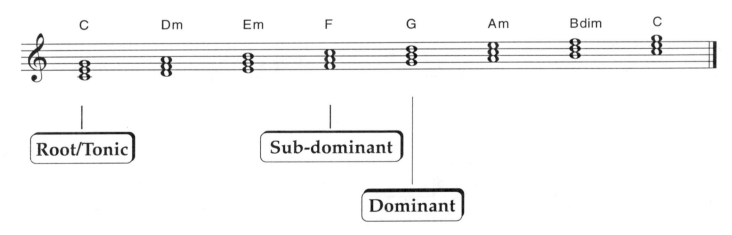

Intervals

The distance from one note to another is called an **Interval**. By combining intervals we can create different sounding chords. When you play notes in a series of intervals you create a melody. Since chords and melodies are built on intervals it is good to know what they are and how they sound.

There are 12 basic intervals in Western music

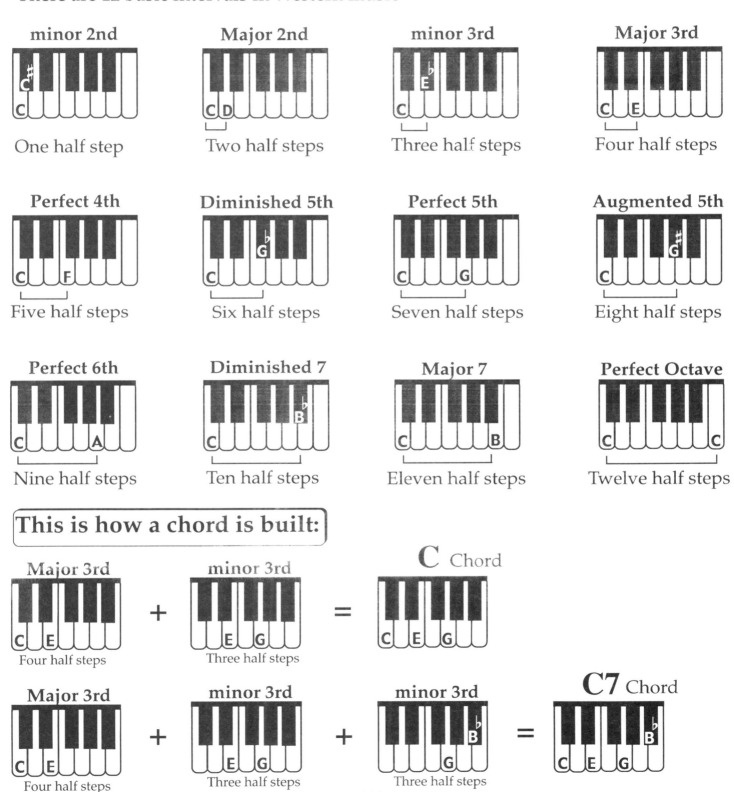

| minor 2nd | Major 2nd | minor 3rd | Major 3rd |
| One half step | Two half steps | Three half steps | Four half steps |

| Perfect 4th | Diminished 5th | Perfect 5th | Augmented 5th |
| Five half steps | Six half steps | Seven half steps | Eight half steps |

| Perfect 6th | Diminished 7 | Major 7 | Perfect Octave |
| Nine half steps | Ten half steps | Eleven half steps | Twelve half steps |

This is how a chord is built:

Major 3rd + minor 3rd = **C** Chord
Four half steps   Three half steps

Major 3rd + minor 3rd + minor 3rd = **C7** Chord
Four half steps   Three half steps   Three half steps

Lead Sheet and Chord Sheet
Practical application of this book

When you go down to your local music store and pick up the sheet music to your favorite song, it will probably look like the example below. What you see is a piano arrangement that someone has written. If this is too hard for you to read, or if you want to make up your own arrangement, you can use the chord symbols above the staff. If you know the melody and words of the song you can accompany yourself by using the chords you have learned in this book. This makes for a great musical experience, much like when somebody picks up a guitar and plays along with their singing.

You can also use the book as a dictionary of chords. If you run across a chord that you don't know, or are not sure how to play, look it up in this book and practice it with the song.

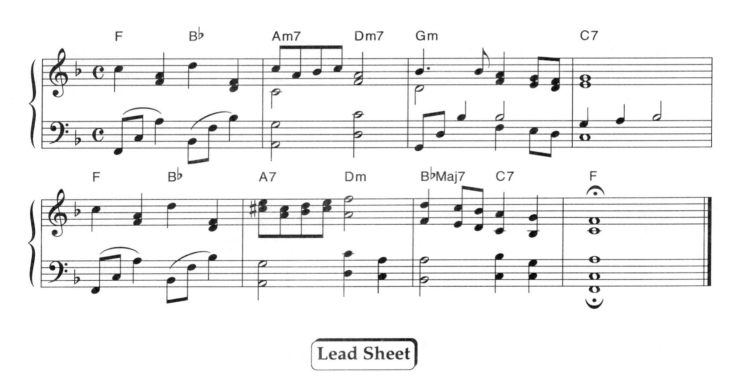

Piano Arrangement With Chords

Lead Sheet

This is the same song but without the full two stave piano arrangement. When you see this type of lead sheet you must use the chord symbols above the staff to make up, or improvise the accompaniment. This type of lead sheet is very common.

Rhythm Sheet

The rhythm sheet is also a common way of displaying chords. All it gives you is the rhythm and chords. The slashes indicate one beat each. Since the song below is in 4/4 time, there are four slashes in each bar. The rhythm sheet works well if you already know the words and melody or if the person you are accompanying knows the song.

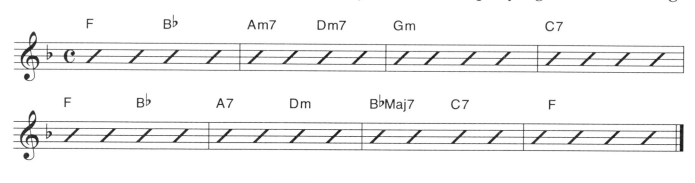

Rhythmic Notation

When indicating a more detailed rhythm, rhythmic notation can be used instead of slashes. It can also exist in combination with slashes. This is an excellent way of showing you rhythms that are important to the song. In rhythmic notation, regular note heads are replaced with diamond or slash shaped symbols. Their note values are the same as regular notation.

Whole Note----4 beats

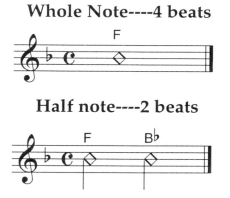

Dotted Half Note----3beats

Half note----2 beats

Eighth Notes----1/2 beat

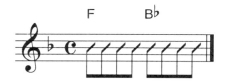

Quarter Note----1 beat

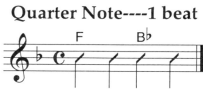

This rhythm sheet shows you a combination of slashes and rhythmic notation.

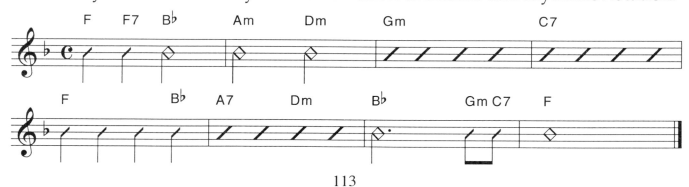

Work Sheets

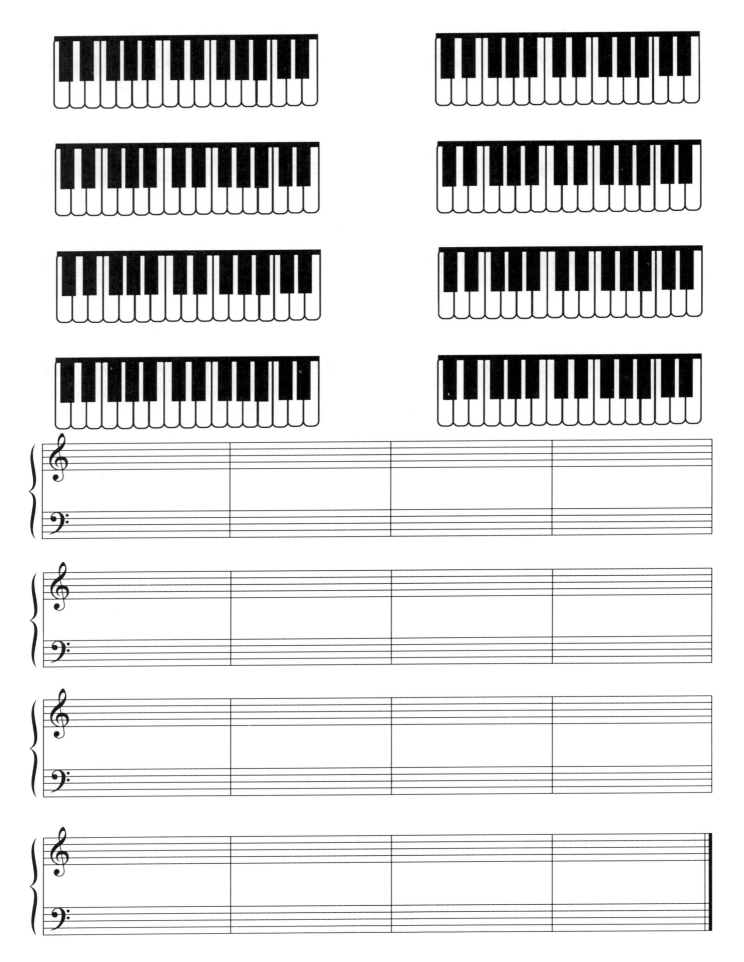

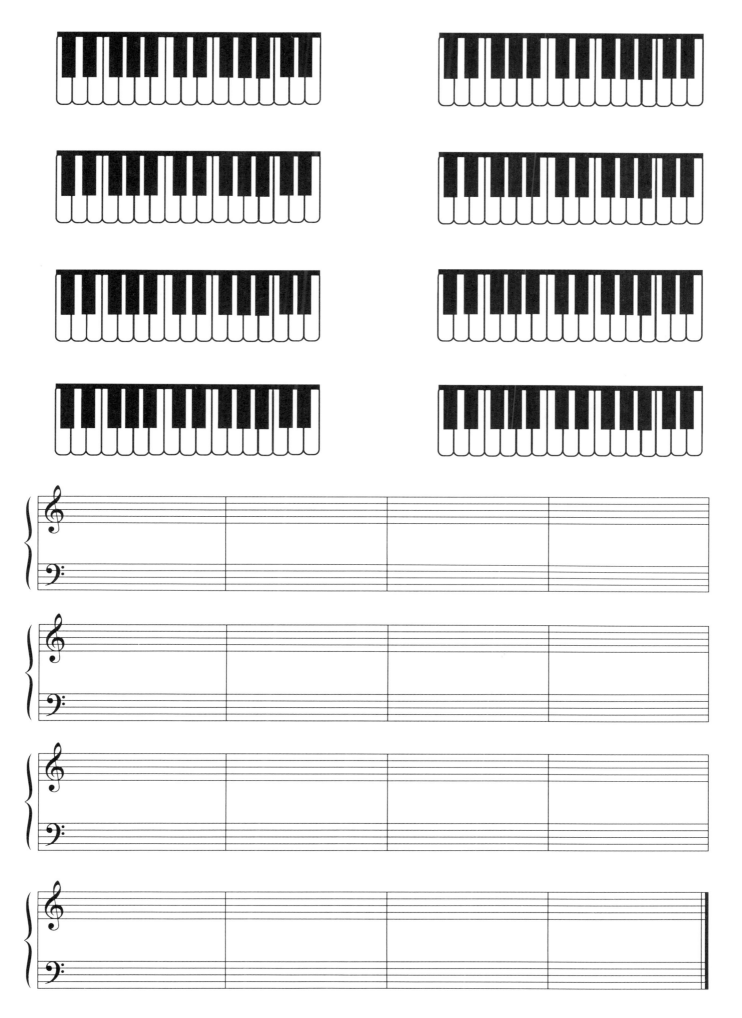

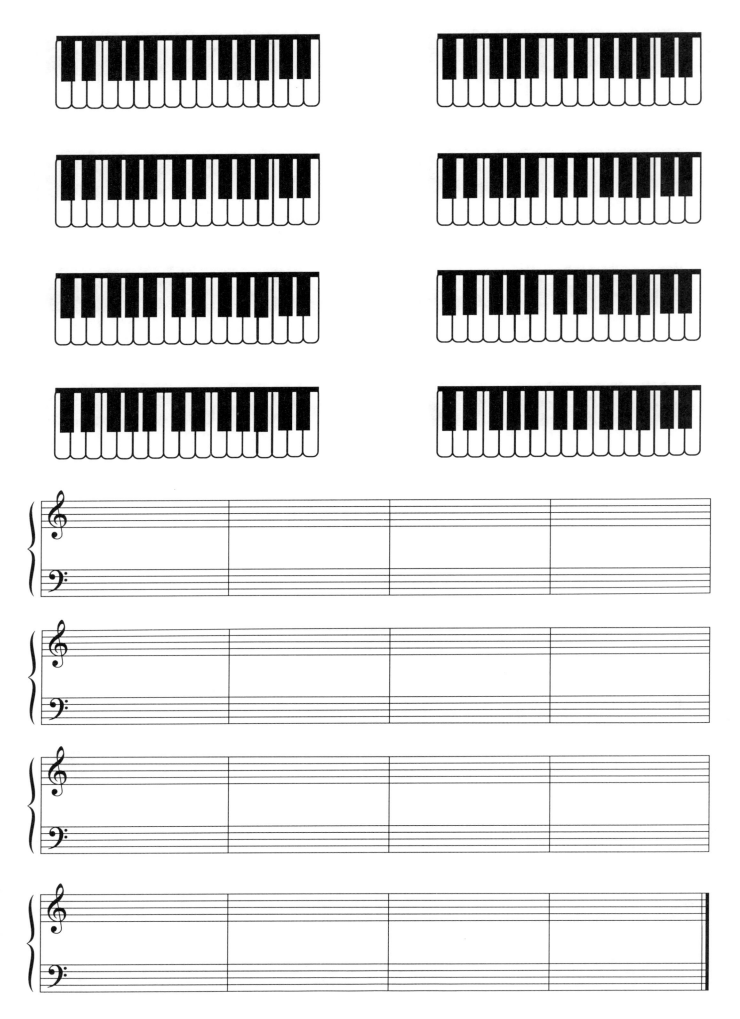

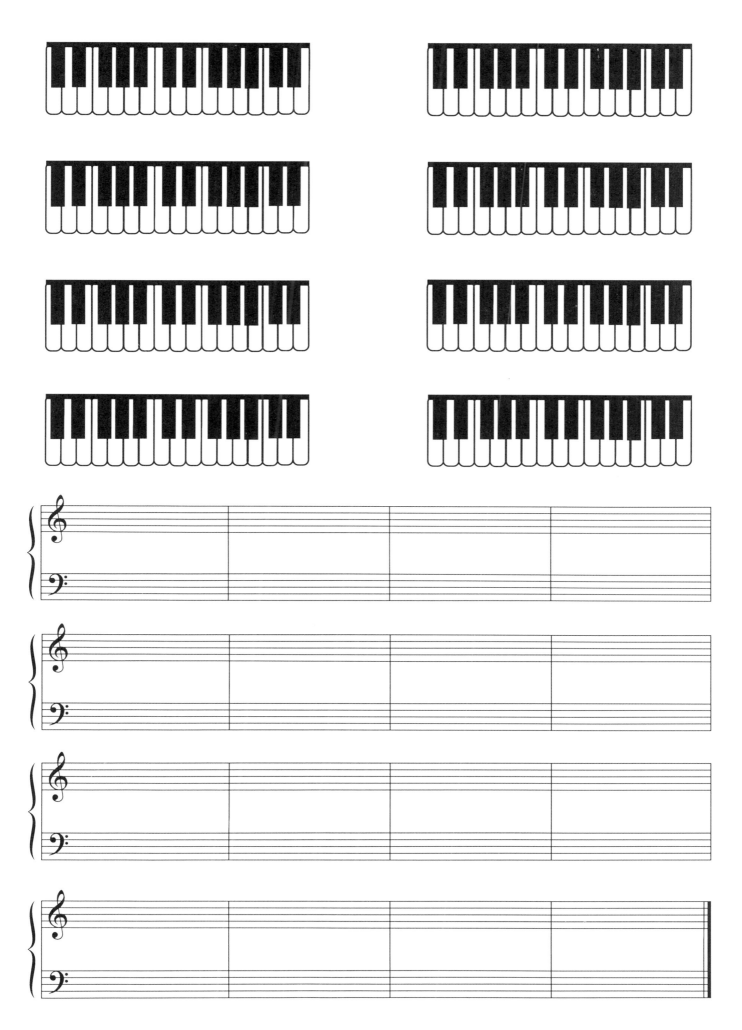

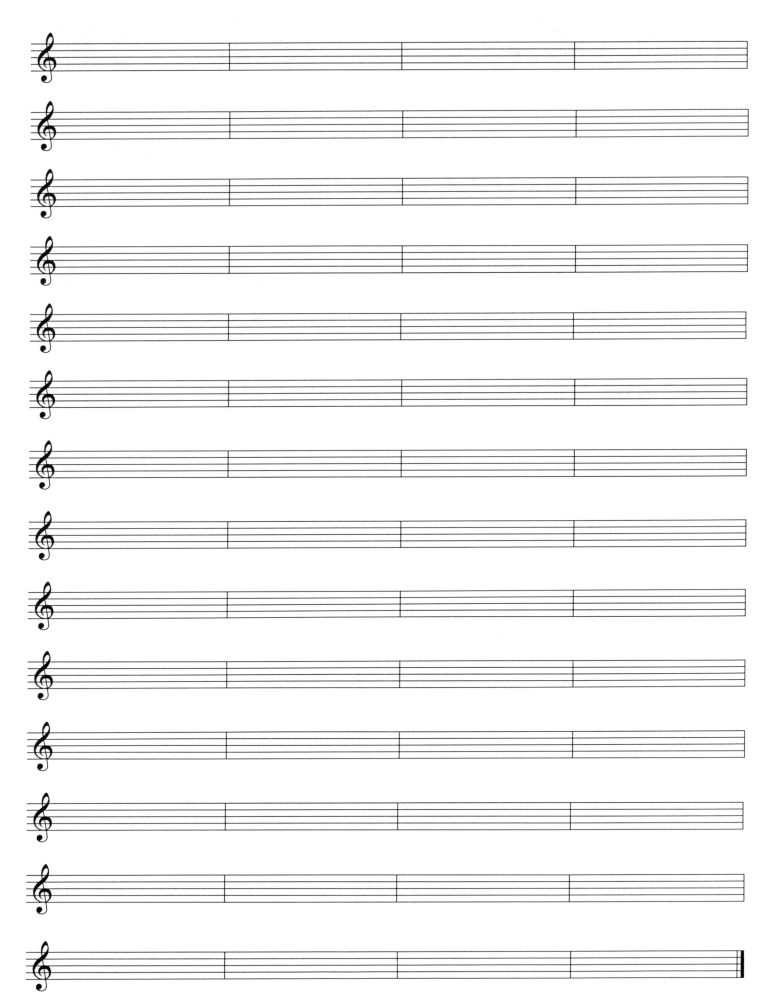

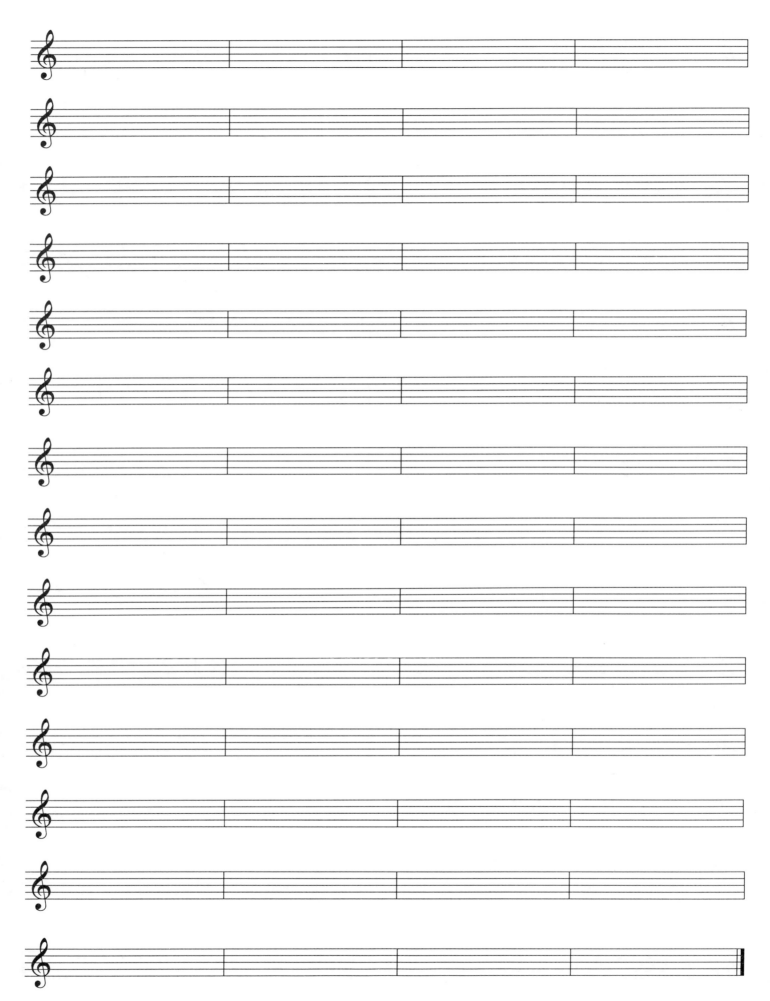